The POWERFUL PANELIST

EVERYTHING YOU NEED TO KNOW TO BE CAPABLE AND CONFIDENT DURING A PANEL DISCUSSION

KRISTIN ARNOLD

QPC Press

Published by QPC Press
Scottsdale, Arizona

Copyright 2023 Kristin Arnold

All rights reserved.

No part of this book may be used or reproduced in any form or by any means, or stored in a database or retrieval system, without prior written permission of the publisher except in case of brief quotations embodied in articles or reviews.

For ordering information or special discounts for bulk purchase, please contact QPC Press at 28150 N. Alma School Parkway, Suite 103-616, Scottsdale, AZ 85262, 800.589.4733.

First printing 2023
ISBN: 979-8-9883440-0-1
Library of Congress Cataloging-in-Publication Data
1. Business communication
2. Business presentations
3. Public speaking

DISCLAIMER

This book is designed to provide basic information about panel discussions. It is not the purpose of this book to reprint all of the information that is otherwise available on the vast subject of panel discussions, but to complement, amplify and supplement other professional journals and books. You are urged to read other available references, learn as much as possible about panel discussions and tailor the information to your individual, team and organizational needs.

The author and QPC Press shall have neither liability nor responsibility to any person or entity with respect to any loss or damage caused, or alleged to be caused, directly or indirectly, by the information contained in this book.

If you do not wish to be bound by the above, you may return this book to the publisher for a full refund.

CONTENTS

FOREWARD iv

INTRODUCTION v

CHAPTER ONE   THE INVITATION...1
What is a panelist? • What role am I expected to play? • Why should I be a panelist? • What if I can't make it to the panel? • Will I get paid to be a panelist? What kind of mindset do you need?

CHAPTER TWO   THE PREPARATION 9
What should I know to prepare? • What is the structure of a typical panel? • How do I prepare for the panel? • Should I practice for the panel? How will I be introduced? • Will I have to give a presentation? • Should I care about speaking order? • How do I promote myself well? • How can I help promote the panel? • How do I craft a compelling story? • What is a good way to share numerical data? How do I make a good impression? • How can I be memorable? • Can we have fun on a panel? • Should I use humor on a panel? • Can I use profanity? • Will I get the questions in advance? • Will I be able to use slides? • Should I prepare a handout or takeaway? • Should I bring a prop? • What should I wear? • Is it okay to wear a costume? • Where should I sit? • Can I invite a friend?

CHAPTER THREE   COUNTDOWN TO SHOWTIME..51
Do we meet the other panelists before the event? • How can I calm my nerves? • Should I use a microphone? • Should I bring my notes on stage? • How early should I get to the venue?

CHAPTER FOUR   ANSWER QUESTIONS 61
How does a typical Q&A session run? • What is the best way to answer a question? • How do I answer a lame question? • How do I shift the focus of the question? • What if I don't have anything to add? • What if I don't know the answer? • How do I answer the "gotcha" question? • What about the last question?

CHAPTER FIVE   MAKE IT CONVERSATIONAL 73
What makes a good conversationalist? • How do I spark conversation? • How do I engage the audience? • How to take a quick, impromptu poll • Should I use first names or titles? • How do I insert myself in the discussion? • Can I be a good panelist if I am introverted? • How do I disagree respectfully?

CHAPTER SIX   AFTER THE PANEL IS OVER 91
What do I do when the panel is over? • Should I write a thank you note? • How do I get on more panels? • How do I get better?

CHAPTER SEVEN   VIRTUAL/REMOTE PANELIST TIPS..99
How to be a brilliant remote panelist • How to foster a sense of intimacy as a remote panelist • How to spark interest remotely • What to wear as a remote panelist

CHAPTER EIGHT   BIGGEST MISTAKES & BEST PRACTICES...107
Top ten common panelist mistakes • Eleven things a panelist should do • Eleven things a panelist should not do

CONCLUSION 113

ACKNOWLEDGEMENTS 114

ABOUT THE AUTHOR... 115

FOREWARD

Kristin cares about empowering others to create compelling live content. If you want to build your profile through presenting at events, being invited to moderate or becoming a panelist is an excellent avenue to share your knowledge. It allows you to bring your unique viewpoint while building relationships with other panelists and the audience in a deeply human way, through conversation.

Event participants like panels, drawn to these by the promise of lively conversation and fresh ideas from multiple perspectives. Panels are also attractive to event participants as learning is compressed into a small timeframe and we all want to maximize results. Kristin offers real talk on delivering what these audiences need and the key role you play.

Well-prepared moderators and panelists can offer participants a selection of valuable, actionable takeaways and have fun while doing it. Like anything worthwhile, this is a skill that can be learned and that benefits from practice. Investing a small amount of time and effort can reap exponential rewards in terms of your own professional development. This guidebook gives you everything you need to be your best and to shine; and offers the reminder that when we fumble, we will recover. If you only have time for one toolkit, use this book. If you want more, Kristin has other deep tools available.

Content curation is a rewarding challenge. It usually involves a combination of invited presenters and sessions from an open submission process. Often in speaker submissions, individuals feel they have a strong enough story that they should not be on a panel, and they may be right. However, there are many good reasons you may be invited to a panel instead. Every event has a limited number of content spaces and the requirement is to build the most compelling complete program that will attract, inform, inspire, and please participants. A combination of formats is more likely to succeed at achieving this overarching goal.

If you are invited to any role on a panel, take a moment to feel honored. It means the curators have seen you have a point of view and are asking you to contribute to this. It can lead to strengthened business relationships and friendships as you connect with others to deliver a robust session. You have been offered an enviable position that invites conversation both on and off the stage. Prepare for the whole process using the wisdom provided by Kristin and the other experts she shares within this guide.

Now, GO, and enjoy the whole process.

Tahira Endean, CITP, CMP, CED
Head of Programme, IMEX
Author, Intentional Event Design, Our Professional Opportunity

INTRODUCTION

Congratulations! You have been invited to be a panelist on an upcoming panel discussion, but what does that really mean? What have you gotten yourself into? What is expected of you? A myriad of questions are rattling around in your brain. You inherently recognize that there is more to being a powerful panelist than just showing up and sharing your wisdom.

Since you and your organization's reputation are on the line, you searched for and found this comprehensive book to ensure you will do a *fabulous* job as a panelist.

First, I want to thank you for finding this book and wanting to be a powerful panelist. Over the past decade, I have been on a crusade to make ALL panel discussions lively and informative. I have dissected a ton of panels—the good, the bad, and the downright ugly. What I have discovered is that a key ingredient to a panel's success is *you*. Not only what you know, but *how* you share your information and interact with the panel moderator and fellow panelists matters.

This book has been written to answer most (if not all) of your questions. It is not meant to be read page-by-page, but rather, to flip through the book while reading the headline question. If the question intrigues you then, by all means, stop and read the answer! I hope you discover information and inspiration to be your absolute best on the panel.

While I tried to cover most of the questions I have been asked over the years, I may have missed one or two. Perhaps you have a better idea or an answer I did not include in this book. In either case, please reach out to me at kristin@powerfulpanels.com with your question or idea. I would love to hear from you!

Regardless of whether this is your first time on a panel or a seasoned panelist, this book will equip you with everything you need to know to be a capable, confident, and powerful panelist.

Kristin Arnold
Scottsdale, Arizona

CHAPTER ONE
THE INVITATION

The opportunity to be a part of a panel discussion is an opportunity to learn from others, to share your own expertise, and to come to a better understanding of the world and its complexities.

Madeleine Albright
Former United States Secretary of State

Being invited to be a panelist is an honor. Not only do you have the opportunity to share your expertise and insights with a wider audience but you can be recognized for your knowledge and contributions to the field. Being a panelist is a chance to engage in meaningful conversation with fellow experts, learn from each other, and collectively advance the understanding and practice of the topic at hand.

This chapter will help you evaluate your decision to say "yes!" to the invitation because it is the right thing for you and the organization you represent.

WHAT IS A PANELIST?

Let's start at the very beginning (as that is a very good place to start!). You have been asked to be a panelist, so let's start with a definition:
A **panelist** is one among a group of people, typically 3-4 experts or practitioners in the field, who share facts, offer opinions, and respond to audience questions either through questions curated by the moderator or taken from the audience directly either in person, virtually, or remotely.

Ideally, a panelist has been selected because they are **D.E.E.P.**:

DIVERSE. A panel in complete agreement makes for a boring panel. The panelists should have diverse perspectives and backgrounds that can spark a scintillating discussion. They should also reflect the diversity seen in the audience.

EXPERTISE. A recognized authority, news-maker, or thought leader within the industry who possesses strong enough credentials that generate credibility quickly through a bio or 30-second introduction. A panelist can also be a practitioner with firsthand knowledge about the topic and has applied it successfully (or not) in the real world, a stakeholder representative along the value chain e.g. a high-profile end-user customer, an employee, and/or a vendor-partner with knowledge on the topic.

ELOQUENT. Panelists should be good conversationalists, able to express their opinion concisely and take a controversial position on a topic—without being a jerk!

PREPARED. The audience knows when a panelist has just shown up without any thought or preparation. The panelists need to know the overall flow of the conversation and have several key points, examples, and takeaways for the audience. Otherwise, the conversation may degrade quickly.

Panelists are typically invited by the meeting sponsor or organizer, contacted by the panel moderator for initial instructions, and *may* have a meet-up with the moderator and other panelists before to the panel discussion. On the day of the panel, panelists should check in with the moderator at least thirty minutes before "showtime" and be prepared to stay afterward to answer any individual audience questions.

Sounds simple enough, but to do it well takes a bit of thought and intentionality. That is the point of this book. To help you think through all the different facets of what it takes to be a powerful panelist—comfortable and confident in your role on stage!

WHAT ROLE AM I EXPECTED TO PLAY?

In addition to having D.E.E.P. panelists, a savvy meeting organizer may also "cast for contrast." My fellow professional panel moderator and Founder of Extreme Meetings, Brian Walter advises his clients to "cast a panel...create a scene, a 'panelesque,' a movie. You want different characters instead of everybody being the same."

Why is this important? Because the meeting organizer may have selected you to play one of these roles (whether consciously or subconsciously!). If you know your "character", you can lean into that role and be even more powerful as a panelist!

Here are some of the roles Walter recommends you cast:

- **THE SAGE.** The Sage is a combination of Dr. Phil, Judge Judy, and Yoda all mixed together. The audience has probably heard of this person or will be incredibly impressed by their credentials.
- **THE RELATOR.** The Relator is someone just like the audience demographics. The audience is going to relate to them because they are thinking, "Oh my gosh, he or she is just like me!"
- **THE EXOTIC.** This person is strikingly different and brings a unique perspective. The audience will be thinking, "I never thought of it like that before. That is interesting..."
- **THE WILD CARD.** This panelist is an unknown. People have no idea what is going to come out of this panelist's mouth. It could be exciting. It could be insightful. It could be irreverent. It could be naughty. You do not actually know, so every time they speak, they lean in wondering, "What's going to happen?"

If you are unclear as to the role you are meant to play, ask the panel moderator or just assume they are not operating at that level of detail. In which case, just be your brilliant self!

WHY SHOULD I BE A PANELIST?

Just because you were *asked* to be a panelist does not mean you have to *accept* the invitation. Before you respond, understand *why* you would want to be a panelist and the benefits to you and/or your organization.

Here are eight reasons why you might want to say "yes" to the invitation:

1. **GET COMFORTABLE WITH PUBLIC SPEAKING.** Speaking at industry conferences and/or professional events can be intimidating, so being a panelist is a great stepping stone where you can ease into greater speaking opportunities.

2. **RAISE YOUR PROFILE AS AN EMERGING LEADER OR EXPERT IN YOUR FIELD.** "There's just something about being up on stage that sends the message that you are someone with whom to do business," says Angel Investor Mike Peiru.

3. **MEET OTHER INFLUENCERS.** Your fellow panelists are great connections, so reach out to them before the panel and get to know them a bit better. As a result, you will be more confident and comfortable conversing with them on stage.

4. **GET SMART.** Even though you might feel qualified to talk about the topic, you will want to do a little research to get up to speed on the latest ideas and key trends impacting the industry and the particular issue being discussed.

5. **REACH NEW CUSTOMERS.** You now have a great reason to reach out to new and potential customers when you invite them to attend the panel discussion—and to let them know how it went along with a summary of the key points discussed.

6. **BE APPRECIATED.** When you provide tangible ideas and valuable takeaways, the audience will appreciate you. They will remember your name and your organization.

7. **BE VISIBLE.** Mark Suster, partner at Upfront Ventures agrees: "People at the conference become aware of who you are....it serves as a great conversation piece to meet people the rest of the conference. People will say, 'Oh, I saw you [on that great panel discussion]'. It's a free icebreaker at the rest of the conference!"

8. **ENCOURAGE DIVERSITY.** Women's leadership expert Jo Miller reminds us, "Even if you can't see the benefit for yourself, consider this: Panels are dominated by baby boomers, senior executives, and white dudes. There is a very real need for more diverse panelists, in terms of gender, career phase, generation, and ethnicity. The audience needs to see people like you, so do us all a favor and accept when you're invited to be a panelist and, when you're not invited… volunteer!"

Obviously, you have a HUGE upside to saying "yes." When you do a great job, you can come out looking like a star. Even so, you may have an equally HUGE downside to saying "yes" if you are not willing to put the work into it.

Please do us all a favor: Say "yes" to being a panelist only when you see a worthwhile upside and are willing to put the work into making your panel discussion simply amazing!

WHAT IF I CAN'T MAKE IT TO THE PANEL?

If something comes up and you cannot make it to the event, let the organizers know as soon as possible. Reach out to them by email, phone, or any other communication method they provided you with. Do not give up until you have made a connection to provide as much notice as possible so they have time to make alternative arrangements.

In your message, be sure to apologize for any inconvenience caused and explain the reason why you will not be able to attend. If you know of someone who could potentially replace you on the panel, you can suggest their name to the organizers. This will be especially helpful if the panel requires a certain level of expertise or experience that your replacement can provide.

You might have talked about the possibility that you cannot make it in your initial call—in which case you will have a better idea of the best method to communicate, their flexibility to accommodate an emergency and backup plans. Oftentimes, the meeting organizer will have a standby panelist, or they have put enough people on the panel should one drop out, it is not a big deal. However, you never know.

Finally, make sure you follow up with the meeting organizer and panel moderator after the event to see how everything went and to express your gratitude for the opportunity and their flexibility. This will help maintain a positive relationship with them, and potentially open up future opportunities for collaboration.

WILL I GET PAID TO BE A PANELIST?

The invitation should also include any compensation details, whether the organization is offering a fee, expenses, and/or registration for the entire event.

Industry professionals, exhibitors, and sponsors are happy to participate since they are already attending. They are already planning on attending and the organization will cover their expenses (travel, lodging, and per diem) as well as the event registration fee. As for their time, they already get a salary from their organization, so they do not expect much. Although a nice gesture, offering something for their time and expenses is not typically expected.

Industry experts, thought leaders, and professional speakers generate their income from sharing their expertise and expect more:

- **PANELIST FEE.** Many speakers who are often asked to be a panelist have a "panelist rate" which is not quite their full fee, or as an adjunct fee aka I will give a speech AND be a panelist.
- **WEBINAR FEE.** Does the entire panel have to be live, or can you stream the speaker to be "on" the live panel? The speaker may have a "webinar" or "virtual/remote" fee.
- **STIPEND.** A stipend is a small monetary contribution to acknowledge the effort given on the panel. How much is "small"? Typically whatever is appropriate for that industry.
- **LUMP SUM TRAVEL AND EXPENSES.** A stated sum to cover your estimated expenses. This may or may not include lodging and ground transportation.
- **CHARITABLE CONTRIBUTION.** A stated sum to be donated on your behalf to your favorite charity.

If the event does not have a budget, then the above is a moot point unless you really want to participate in the panel. "Compensation" does not necessarily mean money. What else is important to you? Visibility? Recognition? Praise? Access to others?

Here are some ideas to negotiate "equitable value":

- **BARTER.** What can the organization or their sponsors offer that will be of equal value to your fee?
- **SPONSORSHIPS.** Could another company sponsor you to get access and visibility to the participants?
- **ACCESS.** Can they share the attendee list and/or VIP access to the heavy hitters in the room?
- **REVENUE.** Can you make an offer and/or sell books or some other product at the back of the room?
- **A PROMISE.** Can they invite you to speak at another high-profile event for a fee?
- **VISIBILITY.** Can they profile you in one of their publications and/or publish an article in their magazine or newsletter?
- **PUBLICITY.** Can they arrange for on-site interviews with the local media?
- **VIDEO.** Ask if they have the internal resources to professionally record the session. (Good video footage is *very* hard to come by and can be extremely costly.)

Bottom line: You need to feel good about the deal you have made. A good deal has a fair exchange of value for you to show up and do your best work as a powerful panelist.

WHAT KIND OF MINDSET DO YOU NEED?

Once you agree to the invitation, shift into a powerful panelist mindset. Executive coach Pam Fox Rollin and I agree on these five essential elements of a powerful panelist:

1. **PASSION.** A panelist must have passion for the topic as an expert, authority, or practitioner in the field. Passion creates energy and virtually compels the audience to lean forward to listen to what they have to say.
2. **GENEROSITY.** A generous panelist willingly shares information, accolades, and perspectives with the other panelists and the audience. Rollin says, "They are willing to share the stuff that matters. As an executive, they may not be able to share *everything*, but they can be generous with little bits of insight that the audience will appreciate."
3. **CURIOSITY.** A panelist should be curious about the other panelists—who they are, what they have to say about the topic, and where they agree and disagree. Although they have passion about the topic, they do not assume they are correct about everything all the time. A powerful panelist is willing to learn something from their fellow panelists. (Pam likes to ask each of the panelists, "What did you learn here today?" as her closing question to the panel discussion).
4. **PROVOCATIVENESS.** A panel where everyone agrees makes for a boring panel. A panelist must be willing to address the tough issues the audience really wants to know, think, or feel. You do not have to act like a panelist on CNN or Fox News, but you should be able to respectfully discuss the key issues.
5. **KINDNESS.** A panelist should be kind. Being able to disagree without being disagreeable. Be respectful of the audience, even when they ask a subjectively stupid question. Respect the audience and their decision to come to listen to you and recognize that they do not have to stay there. Give them a reason to stay and make it a worthwhile investment

Finally, keep in mind that this is not a *chit-chat* among colleagues. It is a *performance* that can (and most probably will in some sort of digital footprint) live beyond the actual event. Being in the correct frame of mind as you prepare for and perform for the panel is essential.

CHAPTER TWO
THE PREPARATION

*A panel discussion is only as good as the preparation that goes into it.
Take the time to research, prepare and rehearse,
and you'll be more than halfway to a successful discussion.*

John C. Maxwell
American author, speaker & pastor

Just as an excellent dinner party requires an overall theme, marvelous guests, and careful planning before the party starts, so does an excellent panel discussion. Just like a fabulous party, the secret sauce is in the planning before the first guest arrives.

For panel discussions, the responsibility falls not only to the host (the meeting organizer) but also to the panel moderator and the panelists themselves. It is the collaboration and preparation between these parties that make a panel powerful.

This chapter will help you prepare for your panel discussion, enabling you to be capable and confident in your role as a powerful panelist.

WHAT SHOULD I KNOW TO PREPARE?

Once you agree to serve on a panel, have a quick conversation with the meeting organizer and/or panel moderator to confirm the event details not mentioned in the invitation. If they have not contacted you after a brief period of time, take the initiative to reach out to them *before* the event. At the very least, they will be delighted you are being so proactive (a rarity, to be sure!). This will allow you to prepare far more effectively by understanding their expectations and how they intend to run the session.

Here is a detailed checklist for you to discuss with the meeting organizer and/or panel moderator:

EVENT DETAILS

- **THE EVENT.** The panel discussion is typically one session within an entire event. Determine where the panel is situated in the event agenda, and what comes before and after the panel discussion. Take a look at the event website and marketing materials. Does the event have a theme? How does the panel fit into the entire agenda?
- **SPONSORING ORGANIZATION.** Review the mission of the business, association, or organization that is hosting the event and/or panel. What are their goals for the panel? Ask about their past experiences of having panels on their program—the good, the bad, and the ugly.

PANEL DETAILS

- **PANEL DATES, START AND END TIMES, AND LOCATION.** Block this day on your schedule and plan to get to the venue well ahead of the start time.
- **PANEL TITLE, TOPIC, AND OBJECTIVES.** Clarify the stated objectives for the panel—especially if marketing material has already been published. What do the organizers want the audience to know, feel, or do about the topic?
- **CONTEXT.** Why did the organizers select this topic? Why are we having this discussion *now*?
- **SCOPE.** Especially when the topic is in a heavily regulated industry or sensitive subject, ask about the scope and boundaries of the topic.
  - Is the intent to dig deep or keep it superficial?
  - What are the guardrails to the discussion? Anything off-limits? Words or phrases to avoid?
  - What is the position of the other panelists?
- **PANEL FORMAT.** Understand their vision for the panel. More presentation or discussion? How formal or informal? Traditional or more unique? Structured debate or conversational? Opinion or evidence-based?
- **PRESENTATION.** Will you be required to provide a brief presentation as part of the introduction or will the format go straight into discussion? If expected to give a presentation, will you be allowed to use supporting slides?
- **MODERATOR STYLE.** Does the moderator prefer more control over the questions or a more conversational approach allowing interruptions and counterpoints?

- **PANEL QUESTIONS.** Will you be given a list of questions the moderator intends to ask?
  - Is the panel moderator interested in getting a list of potential questions?
  - At the very least, what are the first one or two questions they intend to ask?
  - What will be the final question?
  - How will the audience be allowed to ask questions? Anytime or at the end?
  - Will they call on specific panelists to answer specific questions and/or are you expected to jump with questions to the entire panel?
  - Is there an expectation that questions should be answered in a specific amount of time e.g. two minutes? Will there be a timer system? (e.g. a visible timer or colored cards?)
- **AUDIENCE.** Ask for the audience demographics and estimated size so you can tailor your comments and bring the appropriate number of handouts, books, etc.
  - What is the expected level of expertise in the room around the panel topic? Beginner? Moderate? Seasoned veteran?
  - What are the types of organizations and positions that will be represented in the room? (Can you take a peek at the invitee list?)
  - Why do you think they are attending the event and/or panel?
  - What are their key interests, needs, and concerns?
  - What questions are they hoping to be answered?
  - What will be the impact of the panelists' comments on their work and lives?
- **PANELISTS.** Get the names, short bios, and website information for invited panelists and why they were selected.
  - What is the point of view they are likely to contribute to the panel?
  - What role are you expected to play? The Sage? Relator? Exotic? Wild Card?
  - Is there a specific point of view you expect me to take/share?
  - Do not presume you can connect with other panelists via email, LinkedIn, or other platform—ask.
- **GROUND RULES.** Are there any specific ground rules or expectations about how you want this panel to run? How can we best support each other?

- **SUCCESS CRITERIA.** Ask about who and how they will determine and evaluate the success of the panel. Evaluation forms? Hallway buzz?

PANEL LOGISTICS

- **HONORARIUM/TRAVEL.** If applicable, how and by when do they want you to submit the invoice and/or expense receipts?
- **ROOM LOGISTICS.** In order for you to dress accordingly, what is the room size and layout, platform configuration, lighting, and color of the backdrop? What is the furniture configuration, type of chairs, table, water, and expected temperature in the room? How will the panelists get on and off the stage?
- **TECHNOLOGY.** Will we be using any type of technology (e.g. a polling app or ability to crowdsource questions)?
- **MEETING STAFFER.** Will there be a staff person in the room should we need anything? How do we identify them (usually a specific color shirt)?
- **GREEN ROOM.** Will there be a "green room" to meet up before the panel discussion?
- **A/V SUPPORT.** Will there be a professional A/V technician? Will we be using the internal house system?
- **MICROPHONES.** What kind of microphones will we be using? (This may affect what you choose to wear as lavaliere microphones need a place to clip the microphone and the belt pack).
- **PRESENTATIONS.** Ask for specific instructions and restrictions on slides, e.g., time frames, slideshow format, getting the slideshows to them, etc.
- **PROMOTION.** Offer to help get the word out to promote the panel. Who and/or how will the panel be promoted? What is the social hashtag? Are there any expectations to participate in interviews? Podcasts? Other PR?
- **SELF-PROMOTION.** Get a clear understanding of the degree to which you can promote yourself, a product or service, as well as use of social media.
- **RECORDING.** Ask if the panel will be recorded (audio and/or video) or live-streamed. If yes, ask for a form to grant digital rights and a digital copy or link to replay (only if you want to give them the rights to record).
- **ATTIRE.** What is the expected attire/dress for the conference? Is it business, business casual, or casual?
- **MAKE-UP ARTIST.** Will there be a make-up artist and/or hairstylist?
- **CONTINGENCIES.** Discuss various issues or problems that may arise. Consider the "if this, then that" and have a plan:

- o If we start late, are we going to end on time or use the full allotment of time?
- o How do I signal the moderator I want to talk?
- o If the A/V and/or power goes out, what is our backup?
- o What if I have to cancel at the last minute?
- o Other potential concerns or scenarios?

ADDITIONAL REMOTE PANEL LOGISTICS

- **PLATFORM.** What is the technology platform we will be using? Is there a designated "green room" before we go live?
- **TECHNOLOGY DRY RUN.** Will there be a meet-up so we can test the camera, audio, lighting, backgrounds, etc.?
- **REMOTE AUDIENCE ENGAGEMENT.** Will those viewing from remote locations be able to ask questions, chat with themselves, etc.?

MODERATOR MEET UPS

- **PRE-EVENT CALL.** Will there be a short conference or video call to allow everyone to connect and hear the same information?
- **QUICK MEET UP.** Where do you register? Will there be a meet up prior to the start to review the format and discuss any last-minute issues?

From this conversation, you should have a firm grasp on all the logistics, as well as why you were selected, your role, and the flow of the panel. As a result, there will probably be some things you need to deliver to the meeting organizer and/or panel moderator:

- Your photo and short bio to include in promotional materials
- A brief, interesting, and relevant introduction (three sentences)
- Your list of potential questions about the topic

Access a handy panelist checklist at this QR code to help guide the conversation.

WHAT IS THE STRUCTURE OF A TYPICAL PANEL?

The typical panel structure consists of seven tasks that are performed in the following order:

1. Welcome
2. Panelist introductions
3. Panel presentation and/or initial remarks
4. Moderator-curated questions directed to the panelists
5. Questions from the audience directed to a panelist(s)
6. Summary
7. Thank you and final administrative remarks

The panel moderator may opt to do all seven tasks, omit some, combine a few, or design a unique format to achieve the overall desired results.

While the traditional flow of the seven tasks is helpful, think of the tasks in structured "segments" or "chunks." This provides a solid framework to keep the panel on track. For example, for a 30-60 minute panel, there are four common ways to structure a panel discussion:

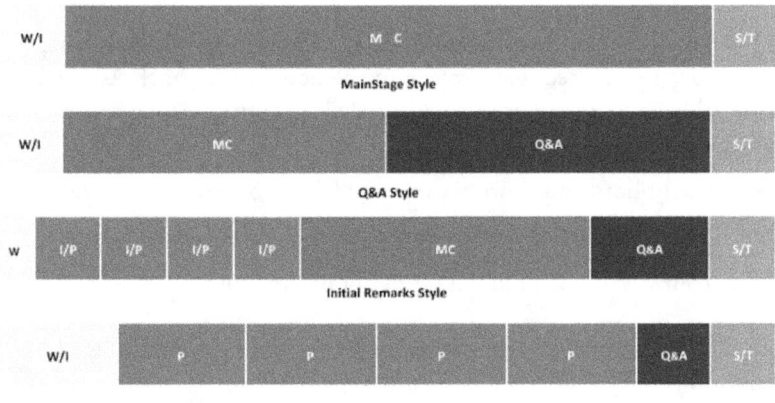

1. **MAINSTAGE STYLE** is a hard-hitting, short-duration panel discussion with panel members; typically the keynoter, main stage presenters, or invited panelists. There is no audience question and answer session (Q&A).
2. **Q&A STYLE** starts with a 2-5 minute introduction of the topic and panelists, 25 minutes of curated questions from the moderator, 25 minutes of audience questions ending with a summary, and thank you.

3. **INITIAL REMARKS STYLE** starts with a 2-5 minute introduction of the topic with each panelist taking five minutes to introduce themselves and their perspectives on the topic. Then 20 minutes of curated questions from the moderator, 10-15 minutes of Q&A with the audience ending with a summary and thank you.
4. **PRESENTATION STYLE** starts with a 2-5 minute introduction of the topic and panelists. Each panelist has 10-15 minutes of uninterrupted sharing of his or her perspective on the topic, 5-10 minutes of Q&A (if you are lucky and the presentations run on time), ending with a summary and thank you.

I must admit, I frown upon the last two structures (the initial remarks and presentation style) as they are more of a panel "presentation" rather than a panel "discussion." Even though most people use the terms interchangeably, they are two distinctly different approaches to a session that has a group of experts sharing their wisdom.

A **panel presentation** is a more traditional approach to having a panel: The moderator introduces each panelist, does some moderated Q&A with the first panelist, then moves on to the second panelist, etc. It is clearly *not* a panel discussion as the panelists are not having a conversation among themselves.

Whereas a **panel discussion** includes time for the panelists to interact with each other—either from the onset or after the panelists' initial remarks/presentations.

This distinction matters most in your preparation. For a panel presentation, you need to prepare…a presentation! For a panel discussion, you will need to prepare key messages as you will be responding to questions, challenging other panelists when you disagree, looking for ways to expand on statements you agree with, and even asking questions of other panelists to get more information.

HOW DO I PREPARE FOR THE PANEL?

Unfortunately, I have seen too many panelists do absolutely NO preparation. They might have read the descriptive email on the flight into the city or briefly chatted with the panel moderator. I affectionately call this the "show up and throw up strategy," where the panelists think they can get by with sheer brilliance.

Unfortunately, it rarely works that way. A powerful D.E.E.P. panelist is willing to do the work. The preparation will give you confidence and a higher degree of comfort, allowing you to be very intentional about what you want to share. It is the difference between just giving *any* answer and the *best response* you can. The work is not a *huge* lift, but it can make a *huge* difference to the audience and their perceived value.

So, what is the work?

- **THINK ABOUT THE AUDIENCE.** After all, they are the reason you are having this awesome discussion.
    - *In Their Shoes.* Imagine the types of people who are likely to attend. Executives? Managers? Front-line employees? If possible, ask to see the invitee list to see what organizations and job titles will be in attendance. Ask yourself:
        - What questions would they like to have answered and/or are likely to ask during the Q&A segment?
        - What compels or drives this group?
        - What do they care about most about this topic?
        - What biases or preconceived notions might they hold?
        - What insights, tools, or techniques might be most beneficial?
    - *Social Media.* Use the conference website, blog posts, social media, or other feedback tools to get a sense of what is on their minds. Ask the audience to submit their most pressing issues and challenges.
    - *Interview.* Ask the conference organizer for the names and contact information of three "influencers" or "heavy hitters" who may be in the audience. Ask them what they would like to hear about and what challenges they are facing.
- **RESEARCH YOUR FELLOW PANELISTS.**
    - *Google* their work and views they hold on the topic. Depending on how much time you have and how critical this panel is, take the time to review their websites, social profiles, books, reviews, bios, blogs, recent presentations, media mentions, papers, etc.
    - *Take Notes.* You do not need to know *everything* about the panelists' lives, but you should have a basic idea of their points of view on the topic. This will make it much easier to connect and converse with them as well as discern the areas where you agree and disagree.
    - *Determine Uniqueness.* From your research, consider what unique point of view you want to take.
- **CONSIDER THE FORMAT.** Is it the typical panel format, or will there be other key areas to engage with the panel moderator, your fellow panelists, and/or the audience?

- **HAVE A GOAL IN MIND.** What do you want to achieve on this panel? Do you want to educate your audience, inspire them, or persuade them to take action? Share new insights and knowledge? Solve a particular problem? Challenge the conventional wisdom?
- **MAKE A LIST OF POTENTIAL QUESTIONS.** Enlist the meeting organizer, panel moderator, and well-informed colleagues to help you identify questions the audience might ask about the topic and your area of expertise. Consider the obvious, most frequently asked questions as well as the not-so-obvious, harder, and more difficult questions that could come up. Plan to cover the most likely questions—and have answers and resources ready in your back pocket, just in case you need them!
- **BE THOUGHTFUL.** Based on your role, diverse viewpoint, and relatability to the audience, determine what contribution you can make to the conversation. Do you have a provocative idea or comment to grab the attention of the audience? If you are wondering if it is too controversial, talk with your organization's legal team about what can and cannot be said.
- **DEVELOP KEY MESSAGES.** Keeping your goal in mind and knowing how best to contribute, identify three to four crisp key messages that speak directly to your audience's interests. You may or may not use all of your key messages, but when in a jam, you will have some "back-pocket" messages to share.
    - *Provide Examples.* Select a concrete and specific example to illustrate each of your points. Personal stories, best practices, demonstrations, and props can help to make your ideas come to life and engage your audience. Your examples should be short, compelling, and easy to understand.
    - *Make the Complex Simple.* Reduce the most complex and technical issues to something plain, simple, and short using the "What? So What? Now What?" structure:
        - What? State your opinion and/or the point you want to make along with a story or an example.
        - So What? Explain why your point is important or relevant to the conversation and audience.
        - Now What? Share the implications, ramifications, applications, and/or recommendations based on your opinion.
    - *Use Repetition.* Help the audience remember the salient points of your presentation with the 3Rs: Repetition, Restatement, and the Rule of Three (people can remember three things, but not much

else). You will want to repeat a key point or restate it with a different approach at least three times.

- **CREATE A HEADLINE.** Anchor your main idea in the form of a memorable theme, concept, or principle that holds your key messages together and remains long after the panel is over. It can be a word, a phrase, a favorite quote, or a catchy "headline" that captures your key point(s) and reinforces a call to action. It could be a recurring symbol or gesture, an acrostic that is easily remembered, or a short soundbite that encapsulates your key point(s) and makes it easier to share long after the panel is done. Encourage your audience to write it down or share with social media to solidify the takeaways and make it easier to share long after the panel is done.

    o *Consider an Acrostic.* When you have three or more points that you want the audience to remember, you may opt to create an acrostic (not an acronym) as a headline to give them an easy way to remember a new system, process, method, or your three points.

    You might be wondering, what is the difference between an acrostic and an acronym? You are not alone as most people confuse the two:

    - An **acrostic** is a word formed from the first letter in each line, or series of lines, that spells a word or phrase when taken in order; for example, NEWS, from North, East, West, and South.
    - An **acronym** is a word formed from the initial letters of a group of words; NSA, for example, is an acronym for the National Speakers Association.

    For a panel discussion, I do not recommend any more than three or four letters as it will just take too long to go through them all. Just make sure you have a pithy way to describe each letter.

- **CALL TO ACTION.** Think about a final takeaway, insight, or idea you want to leave the audience with. I am a big fan of asking the audience to do something like a "call to action" - based on what they heard. Come prepared with at least three different calls to action so you will not be repetitive with your fellow panelists.

- **CHECK WITH LEGAL.** If you are in a heavily regulated industry, make sure you run it through the legal team.

- **OPTIONAL:** Check out the panel moderator. Have they ever moderated a panel before? Just because they are a nice and/or famous person does not mean they have the skills to facilitate a robust panel discussion. If you can, see if they have any videos uploaded on YouTube. How interactive are they? Is their tone conversational? Once you have a sense of their style, you will be better prepared to engage in the conversation.

All of this means doing a lot more work than you signed up for, but if you want to make this an outstanding, powerful panel, you will have a greater chance of success when you do the work.

SHOULD I PRACTICE FOR THE PANEL?

Yes, but you will not practice as you would prepare for a presentation.

Once you have your answers, key messages, and headlines, recognize there are *seven* different moments in a panel discussion where you can share these nuggets of wisdom:

1. During the opening statement.
2. During moderator-curated questions.
3. During audience Q&A.
4. Jumping into the conversation.
5. During closing remarks.
6. Offering a handout or takeaway.
7. Reinforcing your message by posting or engaging on social media.

In determining the best way to get your message across to the audience, brainstorm the possibilities for *each* of these moments. What would that look like in each of those moments? How could you authentically offer your valuable insights?

As in any brainstorming session, you will not execute them all, but a few of your ideas will resonate with you. Practice those specific areas by giving a voice to them out into the world. It is one thing to "prepare" your answers in your head. It is a different kettle of fish to articulate the words that actually come out of your mouth, especially when the audience can instantly broadcast your words via their smartphones.

Without practice, here is what typically happens: You use too many words, you trip over the words, or you do not say what you meant. You want to hone your messages so they are stated concisely and are memorable.

Focus on these three distinct areas to practice:

1. **LIST OF QUESTIONS.** Take your list of prepared questions and push yourself to answer the easy AND the tough questions, ensuring you are giving tremendous value to the attendees. For every question, practice three possible answers from the head, heart, and hands:

   o *Head*: Provide research-based evidence, empirical data, or statistics, especially if you are saying something controversial;

   o *Heart*: Include a personal example, success or lessons learned story, or response meant to motivate or inspire them;

   o *Hands*: Provide practical application or successful "how to" information and approaches.

   Your answers should be concise and provide a bit of interest such as a short anecdote, story, example, facts, or illustration. As you practice, identify those areas you want to avoid or minimize and strategize how you will deal with them if they come up.

2. **YOUR KEY MESSAGES.** Practice delivering three to four crisp key messages that speak directly to your audience's interests. You may or may not use all of your key messages, but when in a jam, you will have some "back pocket" messages to share.

3. **YOUR HEADLINE.** Practice delivering a punchy and memorable "headline" that captures your key point(s) and reinforces a call to action.

Here are some ways you can practice your headline, key messages, and answers:

- **FIND A FRIEND.** Give them the potential questions and have them ask you the question and "role play" how that discussion might pan out for about two minutes. Then stop and ask for feedback: What do each of you think went well and what could you do differently? Incorporate the relevant feedback into the next round. Do this a few times until you feel comfortable with the words, the stories, and your key messages.

- **TALK TO THE MIRROR.** Stand (or sit, depending on your role) and practice some of your answers and stories. At least you are talking to someone and getting your mouth used to saying these words.

- **GO FOR A WALK.** As you are briskly walking, practice some of your answers and stories. You will be amazed at how quickly the time will fly (or walk) by!

- **GO TO THE VENUE EARLY.** Not only can you check out the location, stage, and seating arrangement, but you can practice a few lines to get a feel for room acoustics and ambiance. Make sure you ask the meeting organizer/panel moderator if this is a possibility.

- **NOT AT MEET-UPS.** I do *not* encourage practicing at any of the panel calls or meet-ups as the audience will feel deprived of the spontaneity that happens in the moment. Sure, you can talk about your high-level points, but you want the audience to see the synergy of an unscripted conversation. Otherwise, they will feel like they are getting warmed-up leftovers from previous scintillating conversations.

Speaking of which, you *can* over-practice where the answers are coming out without you even thinking about them. I call this being on "autopilot." I see this with experts who are continually answering the same questions, getting bored with the answer, and being bored with themselves. If you find yourself bored, ask yourself, "What can I do to shake this up, spice it up, and make it more interesting for me and the audience?" I bet you can come up with a few ideas as you practice for a panel discussion.

HOW WILL I BE INTRODUCED?

Since the panel moderator creates the agenda and structure of the panel, they can choose to introduce you in a variety of ways:

- The *moderator can introduce all* of the panelists during their opening remarks. This is particularly efficient when there are more than four panelists and time is of the essence.
- The moderator can ask the *panelists to introduce themselves* giving a minute or two for each to share their credentials and point of view. This also allows each panelist to loosen up and connect with the crowd
- The moderator can ask the panelists to *introduce themselves and share their introductory remarks*—where the remarks are more substantial than a minute or two. This choice is more like a short presentation.
- The moderator can weave in an introductory statement with a *different opening question* for each panelist to highlight the diversity of backgrounds, experiences, or views.
- A panelist *introduces another panelist*. I rarely see this—but it is a possibility.
- If everyone on the panel is already well known to the audience, the panel moderator may choose to *skip the introductions*. They will show a summary slide and get down to business.

If the moderator is introducing you, provide a brief bio that helps the audience understand your credentials and why you have something to add to the discussion. Stick to the essentials in three sentences or less and do not forget to be a little provocative to pique audience interest.

- For example, "To your right (and my left) we have the renowned Kristin Arnold, who is a leading authority on all things about panels. She has professionally moderated over a hundred panels and is the author of three books – all about panels! Something you may not know about Kristin is….."
- If the moderator does not pronounce your name properly, do not make a big deal of it. Just start by saying, "Hello, I'm [name] and move on.
- If the moderator does not give you an adequate introduction, briefly state your credentials and why you are on the panel (in essence the three-sentence introduction you gave the moderator).

If you are introducing yourself, keep it short and sweet. Do not start by thanking the host for having you on the panel (that is a given), fawn all over the panel moderator or fellow panelists (what a waste of time), or go into a lengthy description of yourself, your company, or your latest product. This advice should be obvious, but some people still get carried away in the moment. Do not let that be YOU!

WILL I HAVE TO GIVE A PRESENTATION?

While I prefer panelists *not* to give a presentation, I also realize that some panels are formatted so that the panelists are given a block of time to give a few opening remarks or a presentation. If this is the case, you will want to know how long you are expected to speak, what others are addressing (so you do not repeat them), and if you can (or are expected to) use slides during your presentation.

The invitation might suggest you casually introduce yourself and offer a few "off the cuff" remarks. Right? Please, do not take this task so lightly as your initial remarks will define the audience's first impression of you. It is also the only time you have to make your case without having to respond to a question.

Take some time to create a concise and interesting message that comes in below the specified time limit. If you have given a presentation on the topic before, recognize you may have to choose carefully the points you want to cover and practice this new condensed version. Trust me, the audience will thank you for your precision.

A few things to keep in mind as you practice your presentation:

- **TIMING.** You will probably take longer during the live presentation than during your practice runs, so make sure you time your remarks well.
- **LENGTH.** Be prepared to deliver your speech in a shorter amount of time as it is not at all uncommon for schedules to be adjusted. Perhaps the meeting started late, the agenda item before the panel went longer than expected, or the panelist(s) before you took more time than allotted during their presentations. You just never know what might happen, but you *can* be prepared.

SHOULD I CARE ABOUT SPEAKING ORDER?

The order in which panelists offer their prepared remarks is a major factor in determining how you will be perceived. While each panelist will be speaking on the same topic, your pre-event call should ensure your key points will shed a different aspect or point of view in this segment of the program.

Think about these advantages and disadvantages of being the first, last, or in the middle:

- **FIRST SPEAKER ADVANTAGES & DISADVANTAGES:**
    - The good news about going first is that you will not be compared to anyone—yet. If you are on a panel of several strong presenters, going first makes sense.
    - The first speaker also frames the issue and sets the tone for the entire panel.
    - Since the first speaker typically sits next to the panel moderator, you will benefit from subliminal associative power as the audience looks to the panel moderator for guidance. You will also have easy access to the conversation gatekeeper to signal when you want to interject a comment.
    - The first speaker is typically the panelist to get the first question.
    - Even if the panel moderator loses control of the clock, the first speaker typically gets all the time that was allotted.
    - The disadvantage to going first is you cannot refer to the other panelists in your presentation as they have not said anything yet.

- **LAST SPEAKER ADVANTAGES & DISADVANTAGES:**
  - The biggest advantage of going last is that during your presentation, you can react to and comment on what all the other panelists have said. (Of course, this presumes you have the gift of weaving new thoughts and concepts into your carefully crafted presentation on the fly).
  - Going last also allows you to summarize, rebut what has been said, or propose an entirely different idea.
  - The last speaker gets the last word in this segment.
  - The downside is that you may not have anything else to add, or your time may be cut short if the moderator loses control of the clock.
- **MIDDLE SPEAKER ADVANTAGES & DISADVANTAGES:**
  - The good news about going in the middle is you can comment on what has been said and still shape the discussion for the panelists that go after you.
  - The bad news is you can get lost in the middle. People generally tend to remember things that come first (**primacy bias**) or things that come last (**recency bias**).

Truth be told, most panelists never bother to ask about what position they will be asked to speak in. As a powerful panelist, take the initiative to ask to speak in the best position you feel would place you and your organization in the best light.

HOW DO I PROMOTE MYSELF WELL?

Wondering how the heck you can subtly promote yourself, your product or service, or your organization during a panel discussion? You do not want to be too pushy or too salesy, but there is a reason you said "yes" to the request. Perhaps you are looking for more visibility, or awareness of a new product/service, or organization.

There is a fine line between mentioning your book was just released and hawking the darn thing, picking it up and lovingly petting it like your long-lost puppy, or telling them they would be idiots if they did not come up to talk to you about the book.

Yes indeed, there are other ways to get the point across without you having to shamelessly promote "it"—whatever "it" is:

- **ENLIST THE MODERATOR.** The panel moderator is not stupid. They know there is an inherent reason you agreed to be on the panel—and it usually includes some kind of visibility or recognition. Talk to the moderator about how they can effectively and appropriately promote "it" during the panel discussion.
- **SEND AN ADVANCE COPY.** Offer to send an advance copy of "it" to the panel moderator - they may actually look at it and comment about it spontaneously.
- **THE INTRODUCTION.** As the moderator introduces you, they casually mention "it". For example, they could weave in the fact you are the author of a new book - and maybe even hold up the book for all to see.
- **MODERATOR-CURATED QUESTIONS.** The moderator asks you a question referencing "it" or begs a response you can weave into your answer. For example, the moderator can say, "In your latest book, you mentioned… " or "As an expert in…" or "How might we be able to…"
- **CLOSING.** During the closing comments, the panel moderator can share where to find more information about you, your new book/product/service, or get in touch with you.
- **OTHER PANELISTS** can reference "it" during the panel discussion as well. However, they cannot do that if they do not know about "it." Send them a copy too. During the coordination call(s), share your agenda and what you are specifically looking for. Better yet, call a specific panelist who might help you out. They could say, "You mentioned that in your latest book..." This approach makes everyone look super smart and connected.
- **VISUALS.** A less subtle way of promoting your stuff is a visible representation of "it." For example, you can use your company logo on the backdrop, the product on the tabletop, or a prop as the visual representation of "it"—but only with permission from the panel moderator and meeting organizer. There may be some policies that prohibit this kind of display.
- **URL.** Create a short URL and/or QR code that can be quickly shared with the audience.
- **AUDIENCE.** The audience is not stupid. They know who you are and what company you work for. Provide great value and takeaways for the audience and then you and your company may bask in the afterglow. If you rocked the house, people *will* come up to talk to you.

Instead of shamelessly promoting yourself, your product, or your organization, make your comments in service to the audience. If you have done your job well, they will know and remember who you are and what you do. If they are interested in doing business with you or your organization, they will either come up to you after the panel or be in touch afterward. In other words, serve the audience and let others brag about "it."

HOW CAN I HELP PROMOTE THE PANEL?

Promoting the panel discussion is not just the responsibility of the event organizer. As a panelist, you can help promote the panel to a wider audience, encourage others to attend, engage with the attendees, and follow up after the panel discussion is over.

Here are four ways a panelist can help promote the panel discussion:
1. **SOCIAL MEDIA.** Share details about the event, including the date, time, location, and topic. Use relevant hashtags and tag the other panelists, the panel moderator, and the event organizers to increase visibility. Share the details of the panel discussion on your social media accounts, and encourage your followers to attend or watch the event.
    - *Create Posts.* Highlight the topics that will be covered in the panel discussion.
    - *Make a Video.* Record a short video announcement about the panel discussion.
    - *Engage with Attendees.* Encourage them to ask questions or share their thoughts using a specific hashtag.
    - *Write this Down!* Encourage the audience to post one of your memorable headlines or sound bites.
    - *Recap.* After the panel, share key points from the discussion or highlight interesting insights from the other panelists.
    - *Share Resources.* After the panel is over, share resources such as articles, videos, or other content that expands on the discussion. Be sure to tag the other panelists and the event organizers to help spread the word.
2. **PARTICIPATE IN PRE-EVENT PROMOTIONS.** Participate in any pre-event promotions such as interviews, podcasts, or articles to create buzz around the panel discussion.

3. **EMAIL YOUR NETWORK.** Send an email to your network and let them know about the panel discussion. You can include a brief description of the topics that will be covered and why it is important to attend.
4. **ENGAGE WITH FELLOW PANELISTS.** Reach out to the other panelists and ask them to promote the event on their social media accounts and email lists. Collaboration can help increase the reach of the event.

With your help to promote the panel discussion, you not only increase attendance and engagement but also build your brand and credibility in the industry.

HOW DO I CRAFT A COMPELLING STORY?

Once upon a time....

What happened to you physically as you read those words? If you are like most people, you exhaled; you released the tension in your shoulders as you prepared to read the story.

Stories create the quintessential bonding experience between the moderator, panelists, and the audience. Next time you are at a panel or a presentation, watch how a simple story can bring an audience to life. You can actually see a visible change in the audience when you (or your fellow panelists) tell a story humanizing and personalizing the topic. Most participants will lean forward, smile, and either nod their heads to agree or shake their heads to disagree.

When listeners hear a well-told story, they take a journey with you, correlating their own experiences with yours. Your story becomes their story, or it reminds them of a very similar story from their own lives. Think of it this way: we all have a figurative file drawer containing all of the information we know. It is easier to take in new information when we can relate it to something that resides in that file drawer.

Consider sharing a concise, **personal story** connecting the topic and sparking interest in the audience. Share the impact, benefits as well as unfavorable consequences of your topic on the reality of their lives if the present situation is/is not resolved. Do not forget to choose a few descriptive words using the names of actual persons, places, or events, and give your story an ample sprinkling of color and life.

In addition to personal stories, my favorite types of stories for panels are comparisons, contrasts, allusions, analogies, and examples:

Comparisons show similarities whereas *contrasts* show differences. Use comparisons when you want to reveal similar characteristics, features, and qualities. Conversely, use contrasts when you want to present how one set of conditions differs from another. Some common comparisons and contrasts are:

- IS/IS NOT. This is what it is; this is what it is not.
- RETROSPECTIVE/PROSPECTIVE. That was then; this is now.
- POINT/COUNTERPOINT. Issues for; issues against.
- REVIEW/PREVIEW. Here is where we have been; here is where we are going.

When you **allude** to something, you are making brief, indirect references to a person, place, or event that everybody can identify. An allusion evokes a connection among three parties: you, the audience, and the image you are referencing–without saying who, what, or where it is. Here are a few categories you can allude to:

- POLITICIANS are famous for serving up some phrases that stick. By mentioning a well-known phrase, you make a connection to that time and place in history. For example, "Ask not what your country can do for you, but what you can do for your country" evokes the memory of John F. Kennedy.
- CURRENT EVENTS. You can allude to a current event at a local, regional, or national level. You can also tap into what is happening among the participants' organizations if that information is widely known.
- CELEBRITIES are well-known and thus worthy targets of allusion, even after they are long gone. When I am introduced, my "princess wave" to wordlessly say "hello" to the audience is an allusion to the Princess of Wales.
- CALL BACK. Refer to something that was said earlier during the panel, a question that was asked, or anything that might have occurred from the moment the audience entered the room.

An **analogy** is a comparison of two things to highlight a strong point they have in common. Analogies are often used in technical panel discussions as a way to connect the unknown (what you are presenting) to something the audience already knows.

You can express an analogy in two ways:

- **A SIMILE** compares two things that are not the same and are not normally considered together. The key words you will use when using a simile are "like" or "as." For example, our brains are like a computer. As you read this book, your brain is storing information in your "buffer" just as your computer stores data. What happens when your computer crashes before you hit the save button? You lose all that data.

- **A METAPHOR** is a more direct version of a simile that talks about one thing as if it is the other. Take out the "like" or "as" and your simile becomes a metaphor. To continue the previous example, to retain the information in this book, you need to hit the save button in your brain frequently or risk having an empty hard drive.

Another easy way to spark some interest in your panel discussion is to ask for an example, an illustration, or a demonstration.

You may be wondering, what is the difference?

- **EXAMPLES** are short statements to clarify or elaborate on the points that are usually expressed in one or two sentences. They are often based on your personal experience and prefaced with "for example" or "for instance." When sharing an example, try to refer to specific people in the audience as a whole to demonstrate or make your point.
  An example of this would be "You can easily engage your audience during a panel discussion using a myriad of techniques. For example, you can periodically poll the audience, ask for questions from the audience, or ask a question to discuss in a small group."

- **ILLUSTRATIONS.** When you are looking to extend an example, use an illustration to provide more detail to clarify your point. The best illustrations use specific names, dates, and locations, as appropriate. Generally, an illustration describes a process or chronology of events and provides a level of concreteness that is easily remembered. "Juanita really engages her audiences during a panel discussion. How? Let me give you an illustration. At the panel discussion last week, she crowdsourced audience questions using the meeting app…"

- **DEMONSTRATION.** Whatever your topic, ask yourself these two questions: (1) can I demonstrate "it" (or even a "bit" of "it") for the audience? and (2) better yet, can I create a way for the audience to experience it themselves? Anyone can talk about something in the abstract, however, it is much more interesting to show the audience what you are talking about. Demonstrate the value of your idea right in the moment. A demonstration extends beyond what your audience can see or hear; you can have them taste, smell, or touch an object, prop, or model.

The problem with stories and panels is that time is not your friend. You cannot waste the audience's time with a rambling story that eventually makes the point. Do everyone a favor and practice your stories to ensure they are tightly told and pack a punch.

WHAT IS A GOOD WAY TO SHARE NUMERICAL DATA?

Panelists often spout big numbers to make their point or dazzle the audience with their brilliance. While the numbers are important, it is the understanding of the situation, the emotion it generates, and the feeling the audience is left with that really matters.

Chip Heath and Karla Starr's latest book, *Making Numbers Count: The Art and Science of Communicating Numbers* shows you exactly how to do that. They offer oodles of before and after comparative examples that are highlighted in green-colored boxes throughout the book. The intent is for you to flip through the book, using the highlighted boxes as a springboard to your own creativity.

What kind of tips are we talking about?

- **USE SMALL WHOLE NUMBERS.** The easiest thing to process is whole numbers under 10, preferably 1 to 5.
- **FAVOR USER-FRIENDLY NUMBERS.** If you have to present bigger numbers, round it out so it is easier to mentally process the information. Unless the audience deals in decimals all the time, convert the numbers to whole numbers.
- **CONVERT FRACTIONS AND PERCENTILES TO HUNDREDS.** Fractions force people to do the math. Same with percentiles. Instead, try the "village of 100" or "basket of 100" and convert those percentages into whole numbers.
- **FOCUS ON THE ONE.** Use something simple with a well-understood part of the overall scene: one employee, citizen, or student. one business, marriage, or classroom. One deal, game, or day. Or focus on one concrete chunk of an experience: One prototypical visit, one day, or one month in the quarter.
- **COMPARISONS AND ANALOGIES.** Comparisons help the listener understand the magnitude of a number relative to something they understand and appreciate. Convert and compare it to a concrete object, and recast it into time, space, distance, or money.
- **MAKE IT REAL.** Tie the number to a vivid or emotional connection.

Heath and Starr's book underscores the work, thoughtfulness, and creativity it takes to express a number (or set of numbers) in a meaningful and memorable way. Should you need to make numbers count on your panel discussion, you might want to pick up their book for more ideas.

HOW DO I MAKE A GOOD IMPRESSION?

You walk out on stage, you sit down, and without even saying a word, people think they already know something about you! Unfortunately, very powerful unconscious biases are either working for you or against you.

There are around 185 different unconscious biases possibly working against you. For example, take the **confirmation bias**. People are looking for confirmation. If they see something sloppy in you, they are going to find that sloppiness later in your behavior: how you sit on your chair, how you talk, and the materials/handouts you provide.

To overcome these biases and make a great first and lasting impression, international keynote speaker and colleague Sylvie di Giusto encourages you to prepare for four different types of people you serve when you walk out onstage:

1. **YOURSELF.** Confidence is your best designer. Do not wear, behave, or communicate in any way that makes you feel uncomfortable. Twenty years ago, there were "rules" like you had to wear a suit to be perceived as professional. Do not force yourself into a navy blue, charcoal gray pinstripe suit unless that is your preferred style.

2. **YOUR HOST.** You not only represent yourself, but you also represent the person who invited you to be on the panel. Their reputation is also dependent on you. Find out what expectations your host may have regarding appearance, behavior, or communication.

3. **THE AUDIENCE.** You do not want to be known first and foremost for your outfit or your hairstyle or your makeup. Rather, you want to be known for your excellence, your knowledge, and the added value that you bring to the panel. Therefore, dress in a way that makes you feel confident and in concert with your style rather than make it *the* thing people talk about.

4. **THE A/V TEAM.** Di Giusto says, "Show them right from the beginning you understand that nothing is going to happen without them!" They have very practical information such as the type of microphone, where it will

stand/clip on, what lights they are using, the backdrop color(s), and how colors will appear to the audience (shiny? patterns? contrast colors?), how the audience will view you (on the same level, on a riser, amphitheater/top down, in the round side views?) Di Giusto continues, "I try to make them feel that I care about them as much as they should care about me. It is a give and take and the team will serve you much better and will have much more of an eye on what's happening on the stage."

Di Giusto emphasizes the importance of having a servant mindset: "You serve these four types of people to create a memorable experience on stage. You are not there because it's about you and your knowledge. Unfortunately, we often fall into the trap that it's about us, but it's actually about the guests in the audience, you as a representation of the host entity, with the support of the AV team."

One final thing to consider: Your first impression may not happen on the stage as a panelist. You make it long before when the audience goes to the event website. What picture and bio will they see? Some might even search your name and check out our social media streams. To control the narrative and make a good first impression, submit *worthy* promotional materials and follow up to see what they posted on your behalf.

HOW CAN I BE MEMORABLE?

Two other biases that affect how audiences will remember you: The **primacy** and **recency** bias. The primacy bias is they will remember the first thing they see, the first thing you do and or say. In contrast, the recency bias is they will remember the last thing you do or say.

Most panel moderators will share the first question so you can shine with the first question. But they may or may not share the final question with you. Do not be afraid to ask the panel moderator what the closing question will be and come prepared with at least three different answers. Different possible answers ensure you will not be repetitive with your fellow panelists and can end on a positive note.

Now here comes the zinger: Along with doing the prep work, what *really* makes a panelist or the panel discussion memorable is to do something unexpected and/or something spontaneous. Something they wouldn't normally witness in one of your organization's typical panel discussions.

There is such a thing as "planned spontaneity" where the panelist plans to do something that *appears* to be spontaneous in the eyes of the audience. However, it is not. The panelist has strategically prepared for the "spontaneous" moment relating to the topic of the panel discussion. Doing something spontaneous *just because you can* is just silly.

It also has to be culturally appropriate for the audience. Do not do something that will just piss them off.
You have to be intentional. The most remarkable moments are actually well thought out. Sometimes even rehearsed so you know that it will go well.

Unless you have a very savvy panel moderator who encourages this kind of thinking, planned spontaneity does not happen on its own. Start with a seed of inspiration and see where it takes you by brainstorming ideas with the panel moderator. Join a brainstorming session with one panelist or hold a brainstorming session with all the panelists.

For example, you may want to "spontaneously" call on a colleague who is also Subject Matter Expert (SME) but is not on the panel. You may also consider walking into the audience to demonstrate an idea. Another idea might be to "phone a friend" to provide further insight with the "friend" waiting for your call to prevent lag time.

As you can probably tell from the example, to "plan" spontaneity, think through the possibilities, select one, and meticulously figure out all the little details.

Word of caution: You do not want to blindside the meeting organizer and/or panel moderator, so give them a heads-up on what you have planned.

CAN WE HAVE FUN ON A PANEL?

Oh my goodness, YES! Even though your audience wants to learn something, they are probably hoping to have a bit of fun too!

You do *not* need permission to "bring fun" to the panel. It is not like a lunchbox where you open the fun up and there it is. The key to having fun on the panel is all about your mindset. If you are having fun, others will have fun with you.

Here are some ideas for you to infuse the panel with fun:

- **IMAGINE.** Visualize that you are having the best, most amazing, awesome, and fun panel discussion.
- **ENJOY THE PANEL EXPERIENCE.** Relax, smile, laugh. Enjoy meeting new people, chatting about an interesting topic and even teasing each other in a kindhearted way.
- **COMRADERY.** Meet up and mingle with the moderator and the panelists before the panel to create a bit of rapport among you.
- **FRIENDLY FACES.** Mingle with the audience beforehand. Get to know a few friendly faces and find out what you have in common.

Even with serious and important topics, the audience will mimic the energy of the people on the stage. While it might not be fun talking about unfunny topics, you can still enjoy being with each other, the process, and the conversation.

In my humble opinion, the world does not need another unfun and boring panel discussion, so bring it on!

SHOULD I USE HUMOR ON A PANEL?

A seasoned panel moderator was asked, "Is it necessary to use humor in a panel discussion?" The moderator responded, "Not unless you want people to listen."

Except for the poor person whose car you just rear-ended, everyone likes to laugh, even during deadly serious panel topics. When you make your audience chuckle, they feel more connected not only to you but also to each other. Research has shown that we like to be around people who have a sense of humor. It is a human quality that breaks down tension and resistance and enhances communication and relationships. Plus, it makes the panel more fun!

Now, I am a person who has never considered herself to be funny. Humorists and comedians are funny. My brother is funny. Some of my friends are funny, but funny is not a quality I would use first to describe me.

Truth be told, some people find me witty, which brings a soft chortle, a gleam in the eye, and a smile to the lips. I sometimes get a few chuckles from observational humor and stories that come from my own life experiences. I am just not a laugh-every-six-minutes kind of panel moderator.

I have found ways, though, of strategically using humor to help even the most humor challenged among us. Stop trying to *be* funny and, instead, find ways to engage your audiences with a variety of humor that involves them. Before you know it, you may even be described as funny—in a good way.

Here are a few tips to make humor work for you as a panelist at a panel discussion:

- **MAKE IT NATURAL.** Take the time to understand and appreciate your own style of humor. Stay true to yourself, and do not try to imitate anyone else—unless you are cast as a character to play. Just be you. Everyone else is taken!
- **BE RELEVANT.** Make sure your humor supports the topic. There is nothing worse than irrelevant humor that distracts from the panel discussion.
- **BE APPROPRIATE.** Use humor that is appropriate for your audience, is suitable for the occasion, and is not offensive. While comedians often push the envelope with humor, a panel moderator and panelist humor should engage, not irritate, the audience.
- **ALIGN THE AMOUNT OF HUMOR WITH THE TOPIC.** If the topic is funny, then you will be expected to use a lot of humor. Otherwise, you need to spread your humor throughout to balance out the serious material. After a panel, you never want to hear, "That was funny, but where's the beef?"
- **GO WITH YOUR HUMOR STRENGTHS.** If you can do foreign accents or funny dialogue, then characters might be your humorous strong suit. Be careful you do not offend some group of people. If you have a knack for telling funny stories, then weave away. Though variety is good, you should focus on your strengths.
- **SELF-DEPRECATE.** You are not only the best target for humor but your humor is unlike anyone else's. By creating your own stories and using self-deprecating humor, you create a style of humor that will make you unique. Plus, it connects with audiences and shows how you are not above laughing at yourself and thus are not above them. A little crack in the armor brings you down to earth and makes you more approachable to your audience.

CAN I USE PROFANITY?

Maybe you have been known to drop a swear word or two in casual conversation and are wondering if you can use profanity during a panel discussion.

Years ago, I would categorically say "No." Nowadays, times have changed and the answer is not as clear. Of course, you *can*, but the real question is *should* you use profanity during a panel discussion?

First, ask the meeting organizer and/or panel moderator for their opinion. They have a better sense of their client's threshold for this type of behavior.

Next, consider the audience. Are they prone to drop a few expletives into their normal conversational language? Is it an accepted practice or would it be out of the normal speech cadence?

Also, consider your brand. Media Mogul Gary Vaynerchuk is well known for his liberal use of swear words. If he did not swear, well then, that would be "off-brand" for Gary. Even Gary has a clause in his speaking contract where a client can request no profanity. When in doubt, check it out.

Finally, if the usage of profanity adds to your message, then it is probably okay. If you are just using profanity on a panel discussion because you *can*, then I would reconsider. Perhaps you can use a better, more descriptive word.

WILL I GET THE QUESTIONS IN ADVANCE?

I wish I could unequivocally say, "Yes! You will get all the questions well in advance of the panel discussion!" The reality is you may or may not know the questions in advance. The answer depends on the topic and the panel moderator. Typically, the moderator will ask you about the topic, what questions you are typically asked about the topic, and potential questions for the panel.

Even then you may not know the *exact* questions the moderator will ask. It depends on a few factors:

- **RISK.** With some topics, there is a risk of having a more spontaneous reaction to a question. Especially when there is a lawyer, executive, or celebrity on the panel. Anything they say reflects on them as an individual or as a representative of their organization. Saying something not intended (or permissible) makes it risky.
- **EXPOSURE.** If the session is being videotaped or live-streamed, then the risk factor increases exponentially. Nowadays, everyone with a smartphone is a potential broadcaster, and when you see the large camera at the back of the room, it now becomes an even bigger risk.

- **PERSONAL CHOICE.** Perhaps it is the first time a panelist is on a panel or the moderator is not as familiar with the industry and/or specific wording of the questions. Sharing the questions will make the panelists and/or moderator more capable and confident.

WILL I BE ABLE TO USE SLIDES?

Panel founder and American educator Harry A. Overstreet first coined the term **panel discussion** in a short article "*On the Panel*" published in the October 1934 issue of *The Trained Nurse and Hospital Review*. In that article, he said the "one unforgivable offense is to rise and give a presentation." Since slides are used for presentations, do not use slides during a panel discussion. The focus should be on the *discussion* and interaction between panelists and *not* a humongous screen!

That being said, there can be some instances when one or two of your slides would be appropriate in a panel discussion. Request to use a slide when it:

- Adds value from the attendee's perspective.
- Makes an abstract concept more visibly understandable.
- Grabs the audience's attention.

If you want to add a slide or two, ask the panel moderator plenty of time *before the panel* if this is okay as they will probably want to alert the rest of the panelists they too can submit a slide or two.

From the moderator's point of view, there are some other times when it might be appropriate to have a slide:

- **PANELIST SLIDE.** One slide for each panelist with a photograph, name, a few key bullet points, and social handle. Display this slide when the panelist is introduced. Create a continuous loop of the panelist slides to show as people are walking into the room, and before the start of the session.
- **PANELIST SUMMARY SLIDE.** One slide with each panelist lined up in the same seating order with photo, headline, and social handle. This stays up for the duration of the session.
- **TRANSITION.** A funny, applicable video transition as the panel is getting set up or right after it is over

If you are going to use slides, here are a few tips:

- A 60-minute panel can get through 15-20 slides and a panelist should speak to only 2-3 slides before giving the floor to another panelist. Set a max number of slides and amount of time.

- Keep the slides brief and specific to the topic. Consider having additional information in a handout, takeaway, or on a website rather than in the slides.

- Use the organization's defined format or template, if required.

- Include the panelists' contact names and information on their slides.

- Keep the slideshow from being dependent on Wi-Fi. Although it may be accessible, it may not work.

- Use video judiciously. It can gobble up precious time quickly.

If you must offer a lot of data or supplementary material, give people a link, handout, or takeaway.

If possible, the panel moderator will want to collect the slides early to review them before the event to ensure all the panelists are addressing the topic, limiting their slide count and minimizing duplication among their presentations. Do not worry about making all the slides look the same—unless the organization has mandated it.

The panel moderator and/or the A/V team will assemble *one* overall slideshow file and is responsible for advancing the slide deck.

Finally, DO NOT approach the meeting organizer or panel moderator with a thumb drive to show a slide or video at the very last minute. They do not need the extra stress of your last-minute wishes compounded with concerns about the security of your thumb drive.

SHOULD I PREPARE A HANDOUT OR TAKEAWAY?

Many panelists want to provide more value to the audience in the form of a handout. That is what they *say*, but I am not so sure that is what they *mean*.

A **handout** is printed material supporting the panel discussion. It can be in the form of an agenda, an outline, slide printouts, fact sheets, a list of references, a spreadsheet, or an article handed out before or during the panel. It can also include promotional materials about you, your fellow panelists, their organizations, or a specific product or service that would benefit the audience.

A panelist may prepare a **takeaway**, which is slightly different. A takeaway can be the same thing as your handout, a link or QR code to the handout and/or more supplemental information, or some other gift or freebie. The only difference is that it is given to attendees as they leave the meeting.

Handouts exist to give the audience a way to take notes during the panel discussion. When people write things down, they are also more likely to remember the salient points, even if they never go back and look at their notes again. Handouts also provide audience members with a sense of security, especially during highly technical panel discussions, because they know there is detailed information to refer to if necessary. As an added benefit to you, should your technology fail, you can always rely on your handouts.

Sounds like you should always have a handout, right? Not so fast; Every coin has two sides. If you give the audience material to refer to while the panel talks, you run the risk of losing the attention of a large percentage of your audience. They will be looking at and reading the handout rather than *listening* to the panel. They will also be flipping ahead, trying to figure out what the panel is *going* to say rather than listening to what they *are* saying.

While there is no "right" or "wrong" answer, you do have choices when it comes to using handouts:

- *Email* your handout before the panel discussion. Encourage the audience to download the handout to use during the panel discussion.
- Put the handouts *on each chair* or the table at each place right before people come in.
- Distribute your handout *as people walk in*. The ushers at church do this quite efficiently.
- Distribute your handout *at a specific moment* during your presentation.
- Save your handout for the *end of your speech*. Now it is called a **takeaway**.
- Consider distributing your handout/takeaway and any other supplemental information in PDF format on a flash drive or providing a *web page URL*.

Work with your meeting organizer and panel moderator to determine the best strategy to share this important information. Make sure these gifts have your bio, contact information (including your social media address), and a resource list where the audience can find more information. Finally, remind the panel moderator to tell the audience the strategy upfront so they can know what to expect. Unless, of course, you want it to be a surprise!

SHOULD I BRING A PROP?

Remember elementary school where you brought in an item for show and tell? You can do the same thing by bringing a prop directly related to your passion for the topic.

Simply put, props bring your words to life. You can use props to strengthen your audience's ability to visualize, understand, accept, and remember an idea, concept, or theme during the panel discussion. Many panelists may struggle with this technique, so here are a few examples to help spur your thinking:

- **ENHANCERS.** For a panel about oyster restoration in the Chesapeake Bay, one panelist brought an actual local oyster, another brought in a replica of a non-native oyster, and another brought in a piece of aqua-farming material. Each prop set the context in real-world terms, and they enhanced our understanding and appreciation of the topic.
- **THEATRICAL.** Actors use props to help the audience believe and follow what they are saying. Moderators and panelists can as well. For example, hold up the magazine or book you are quoting.
- **METAPHORICAL.** Metaphorical props are used to make or reinforce your point. For example, show a Slinky® to illustrate the need for flexibility, or a telescoping spyglass to show how strategic, business, and operational plans all need to be integrated.
- **MODEL.** A model is a representation (usually smaller) of an object, person, or concept. Although you cannot bring a bulldozer into the panel discussion, you can certainly bring a toy bulldozer with you. Doctors often point to an organ model as they explain a physiological problem.

In a pinch, ask to show one slide picturing the prop just in case you cannot bring it to the panel because it is too big, too small, too dangerous, or too weird.

HOW TO USE A PROP

1. **KEEP IT HIDDEN.** Keep the prop out of sight until you are ready to use it unless you want to keep the prop onstage to arouse curiosity.
2. **AGREE.** Ask the audience to agree with you on an idea that is connected to the prop. Get them to nod.

3. **INTRODUCE THE PROP.** Introduce the prop to the audience. Hold it in front of you; hold it high and hold it steady. Move it slowly so it can be seen from all parts of the room. Do not talk to the prop. Talk to the audience.
4. **SHARE THE PROP.** Do not hesitate to share the prop with your panelists—even with the audience—if it is not too fragile or valuable.
5. **PUT IT AWAY.** Put it away or out of sight when you are done. Resist the temptation to pass it around. The handoff from person to person and each person's close inspection will be very distracting.

WHAT SHOULD I WEAR?

Ever wonder what to wear to a panel discussion? The answer is not as simple or obvious as you might think. Although you want a textbook answer, several factors must be considered first:

- **THE EVENT.** Is it a formal or informal event? What kind of event is it? (e.g. business, corporate, academic, community, religious. etc.). The nature of the event itself may direct the choices you will make.
- **THE INDUSTRY.** Some industries and/or professions are more conservative than others (e.g. engineering, finance, and law). For example, you can be more stylish with creative industries (e.g. fashion, music, advertising), and more casual with certain professions (IT, sales, entrepreneurs).
- **THE AUDIENCE.** Who will be in the audience and how does the meeting organizer think they will be dressed? Try to dress "one level" more professionally than the audience.
- **THE STAGE.** Will the audience be on the same level/floor with you or will you be on a stage or riser? Perhaps they will be looking down at you in an amphitheater or all around in a "fishbowl" layout. Will you be sitting behind a table or standing behind a lectern? What chairs will you be sitting on? Will there be a live video screen projection? Think about what the audience will see when directly looking at you.
- **THE BACKGROUND.** What is the color of the background? Logos? Images? You do not want to wear the same color as you will look like a floating head!
- **THE MICROPHONE.** What type of microphone(s) will be used? You do not want fabrics or jewelry clanking against the microphone. If it is a lavaliere microphone, think about where you will clip on the microphone and the microphone pack.

- **YOUR PERSONAL STYLE.** International speaker and colleague, Sylvie di Giusto suggests you identify your "style DNA." She has a complimentary perception audit you can access at this QR code.

- **THE VIBE.** You said "Yes!" to the panel invitation for a reason and you have a specific objective in mind. You are also playing a specific role on the panel as you share your expertise. The answers to these questions will give you the "vibe" that you want to convey e.g. smart, approachable, knowledgeable. You want your outfit to line up with that vibe.

When you consider these factors, you will have a better sense of what to wear to a panel discussion. You want your clothing choices to impress yet be unobtrusive as the focus of the panel must be on the content.

GENERAL TIPS ON WHAT TO WEAR

Your audience assumes that you are an expert or leader in your field with important information to share. Therefore, when you walk onto that stage, you want to:

- **FEEL CONFIDENT.** Wear a comfortable outfit that makes you feel good about yourself. Now is not the time to try something new, unless it fits you perfectly. Otherwise, you will be fussing with it.
- **BE UP-TO-DATE.** Outdated clothes may send a subliminal message to the audience that your ideas and insights might be out of date as well.
- **CONTRAST COLORS.** You do not want to blend in, but you also do not want to stand out like a sore thumb. The key here is to think about contrasting colors. Di Giusto says, "If you wear a navy-blue jacket with a blue or a grey blouse—that is low contrast and very difficult for lighting and cameras. Pair a navy-blue jacket with a white or pink shirt that provides high contrast."
- **POP A COLOR.** Add a bit of color somewhere near your face to give your image a bit of intrigue. For instance, add a pop of color with your shirt, tie, scarf, or pocket scarf).

- **FIT RIGHT.** Make sure your clothes fit properly and they are not too tight or too loose. A tailored silhouette gives you instant authority. Kristina Moore, Founder of Corporate Fashionista says, "Ill-fitting clothes instantly send a message to the audience that you may not be reliably attentive to their professional needs or be able to tend to the details of their projects if you cannot attend to the important details of your own professional dress."
- **DO A QUICK CHECK.** Look for visual distractions including loose buttons and threads, visible undergarments, wrinkle-prone fabrics, sweat stains, noisy shoes, and distracting/noisy jewelry.
- **GET INSPIRED.** Watch a few news shows and see what the hosts and guests wear. You are bound to pick up some ideas, especially if you know that you are going to be live-streamed to the in-person and/or remote audience.

Here are a few faux-pas you want to avoid:
- **SHOW TOO MUCH SKIN.** Avoid bare shoulders, plunging necklines, and potential wardrobe malfunctions.
- **STRAIN THE EYES.** Busy patterns, floral prints, or shiny fabrics may clash with everything else going on.
- **WEAR TRANSPARENT FABRICS.** Beware of any fabric potentially becoming transparent under a bright beam of light. The audience may be able to see through chiffon, cashmere, knits, linen, and cotton when thin or pale enough.
- **KNOTTY DETAILS.** Stay away from "complicated" features such as buckles, wrap ties, or weird buttons that may distract or malfunction.
- **BE OVER-THE-TOP.** Unless it is part of your brand, stay away from big earrings, over-the-top necklaces, oversized scarves, hats, dramatic eyeglass frames, or a raft of bracelets.

Remember, you want people to pay attention to what you are *saying* rather than be distracted by what you are *wearing*. Follow these tips on what to wear on a panel discussion and you will definitely impress the audience.

TIPS FOR MEN

- **THE DEFAULT.** You cannot go wrong with a suit or sports coat.
- **TIES.** Wear a tie with a pop of color—or a striped tie. Try to stay away from paisley or big patterns.

- **SHIRTS.** Contrast your jacket with a colored shirt (or a white shirt—but only if it is in your color palette).
- **SOCKS.** Make sure your socks cover your calves, so when you cross your legs, we still see socks and not your bare skin or hairy legs.
- **SHOES.** You would be surprised at how many people look at your shoes. Make sure they are polished and not scuffed with holes in the soles.
- **JEANS.** Depending on the audience and the vibe you are aiming for, dark-blue, well-fitting jeans (that are not ripped or fraying at the hem) can be quite chic.

TIPS FOR WOMEN

- **THE DEFAULT.** You cannot go wrong with a navy blue, dark grey, or chestnut brown pantsuit, especially if the audience is primarily male.
- **COLOR.** Kristina Moore, Founder of Corporate Fashionista says, "Rich, lush, and vibrant colors work best for professional speaking engagements. Blues and greens are always a hit. Plus, these energetic colors will emphasize and bring forth the passion and enthusiasm you hold for the content of your message. Dynamic colors will be inviting to your audience. I am not suggesting that you wear loud neon colors but, rather those colors that are flattering on your skin tone in a bolder tone than you might regularly wear. This way you will be appropriately noticeable in the crowd."
- **BLOUSE.** Contrast your jacket with a solid-colored or subtle pattern blouse. Wear a white shirt only if it is in your color palette). Retailer M.M. LaFleur encourages you to "Frame your face. Details like pretty collars and notched necklines put the emphasis where it should be—on your mouth and the words emanating from it. While a super-low plunge is a no-no, a deep V-neck can draw eyeballs upward to your face."
- **SKIRT.** If you do not want to wear a pantsuit, a pencil skirt slightly above the knee with a jacket that hits at hip level and a cute blouse will do the job, especially since you can clip the microphone pack to the back of your skirt.
- **DRESS.** Some women simply prefer to wear a dress. Make sure the cut is well-tailored, hits slightly above the knee, and does not reveal a lot of skin. You can also top it off with a leather moto jacket or cardigan sweater in a great color. (Do not forget to think through where you are going to put the microphone pack if using a lavaliere microphone).
- **PANTYHOSE.** Unless you have fabulous-looking legs, wear sheer nylons.

- **SHOES.** It is best to wear shoes you can walk in, stand in, and sit comfortably without tripping, stumbling, or looking awkward. The default is to keep the heels on the low side—and watch out for the sound you make as you walk across the stage.
- **ACCESSORIES.** Wear one eye-catching accessory, such as a necklace, bracelet, earrings, scarf, pin, hat, or even shoes to spice up an outfit.
- **LIPSTICK.** Wear a dark lipstick within your color palette that you like and feel comfortable in. Do not use pink or mauve as they provide low contrast.
- **JEANS.** This is trickier for women. Depending on the audience and the vibe you are aiming for, you could sport dark-colored jeans cut like a trouser and not too form-fitting with no visible rips, trims, or stitching. (I have only worn jeans once in my entire career and that was at a JavaScript conference where my jeans were actually a notch above what everyone else was wearing.)

IS IT OK TO WEAR A COSTUME?

Sure it is okay—as long as it is related to the topic, your personal brand, the theme of the conference, or the host company's slogan. Feel free to "dress it up," adding a touch of flair and excitement to the panel.

Here are a few cases where you might what to wear a costume:
- **CONNECT TO THE EVENT.** As part of the event theme, you might be asked to wear something that all the participants might be wearing such as your favorite sports jersey, Hawaiian shirt, or a specific color.
- **CONNECT TO THE TOPIC.** Wear something that is connected to your topic. Frank Kelly started a panel discussion with an example of the power of first impressions. "I wear a suit that's one size too large, have bad posture, and carry a piece of paper. I start, in a very monotonous voice, 'Um, yes. We're here to talk about how to leave a lasting impression.'" Just as the audience begins to fidget and feel uncomfortable, he changes his demeanor and takes off the ill-fitting suit to reveal a well-tailored one beneath.
- **CONNECT TO THE PART.** Perhaps you can accentuate the "part" you are playing on the panel.

- **CONNECT TO A POSITION.** You are asked to take on supporting or defending a particular position and/or opposing a position. In this case, you could wear one color and your "opponents" could wear another color.
- **MAKE A POINT.** Professional speaker and internet marketer Tom Antion tells a story about moderating a panel of senior managers of a pizza franchise. "I asked one of the panelists to march into the meeting wearing a filthy doctor's lab coat with ketchup all over it to represent fake blood. I had another panelist come in with a crisp, new lab coat. I asked a simple question: 'Which manager would you like operating on you?' Of course, all the junior managers yelled out they wouldn't let either one of these people operate on them. Everyone was laughing and joking around, but the point was made. They must keep their employees looking clean and neat because nice customers won't want to be served by grungy food service workers."
- **PLAY A CHARACTER.** The ultimate visual combines all these techniques to become a "character" within your presentation. Dress up to be seen as the expert, the relator, the exotic or the wild card! During a heated panel discussion with author Sasscer Hill, the panel moderator came dressed in a referee shirt, hat, and whistle. He proceeded to moderate the panel as if he was the referee at a soccer match!

All it takes is a little inspiration and ingenuity to create a little visual excitement at your panel discussion.

WHERE SHOULD I SIT?

Ideally, the panel moderator briefed you before the panel discussion about the room logistics: The stage, the chairs, and where you will be sitting amongst the panelists. They may even have a slide projecting all the panelists' names, social handles, and pictures, all in the order in which you are seated.

Don't hold your breath, though. You may end up with a disorganized, lackadaisical moderator who says, "Go ahead and sit wherever."

If that is the case, arrive early enough to walk onto the stage and claim the best chair in the house. Place your notes, clipboard, or another piece of personal property on the chair.

What, exactly, *is* the "best chair" for a panelist? Well, that decision should align with your objectives for saying "yes" to being a panelist:

- **POWER.** Sit next to, preferably to the right of the panel moderator. This puts you in view as people look at the leader of the panel and a subliminal connection is made. You will also have easy access to the conversation gatekeeper.
- **NETWORKING.** Your fellow panelists are great connections, so you not only want to reach out to them *before* the panel and get to know them a bit better, but you will want to sit next to them as well. Similar to the panel moderator, you will want to sit to the right of the person you want to know better.
- **AFFILIATION.** Sometimes, your objectives go beyond networking. You want to be seen as closely affiliated with another highly influential panelist. In that case, you want to sit to the right of that highly influential person.
- **INFLUENCE.** Let's say you are the most influential person on the panel. You want to claim the middle seat. Why? Because people subconsciously gravitate to the person in the middle as the most influential one.
- **BUILD TRUST WITH ANOTHER PANELIST.** Sit to the right of a person when you want to generate a feeling of trust. In medieval times, people of questionable loyalty were seated on the left because right-handed people would normally thrust a dagger to the left! Hence, we now have the term "right-hand man."
- **DISCUSSION.** Choose the "central seats" (those at the ends and the middle seats) when you want to be actively involved in the meeting discussion.
- **CONFRONTATION.** Sit the furthest away from the panelist who, you believe, has an opposing view or recommendation. This will make any differences of opinion include the rest of the panel and will keep it from looking like two people bickering.
- **DIVERSITY.** Take a look at the panelist lineup. Are all the women on one side and the men on another? Select a chair to mix up the visual diversity of the panel.
- **EXIT.** Sometimes, life gets in the way of your panel discussion: you are not feeling well or expecting an urgent and important call from a loved one and need to make a quick escape. If so, sit closest to the door in the event you need to make a quick exit.

Finally, when you do not have a compelling reason for choosing one seat over another, sit wherever you are most comfortable on the stage.

Once you decide on the "best chair," take a moment to situate yourself:

- **TEST YOUR CHAIR.** Make sure the chair is set at the right height, and adjust the height or footrests as necessary.

- **SIT UP TALL.** Trevor Currie at Podium Consulting says, "Avoid the temptation to sink back into your chair. This contracts your diaphragm and reduces your presence. Be conscious of your posture and sit closer to the front of your seat and rest your forearms on the table when you are not using your hands" if you are sitting in front of a table.
- **LOCATE THE MICROPHONE.** There are several microphone setups for a panel discussion. Find the audio-visual technician or ask the meeting organizer about the microphone, if applicable.

After you check in with the meeting organizer and the panel moderator, and scope out the stage and chair, go mingle with the audience in the few minutes before the panel starts.

CAN I INVITE A FRIEND?

Inviting a friend to attend your panel discussion is a great idea, just check with the meeting organizer first. There may be some reason why you cannot. For example, they are at the max number of people in the room, the event is exclusive, or they do not want to have to feed another mouth. Do not assume it will be okay.

If they say, "Yes," having a friend or two in the room can be super helpful. Just be clear they are there to support YOU as they may have their own agenda and completely forget about why you invited them to come along!

Here are a few ways your friends can help you be successful during a panel discussion:

- **BE YOUR CHEERLEADER.** You will have at least one or two smiling, familiar faces out in the audience. If you are nervous, remember they are cheering you on!
- **TAKE PICTURES.** Even though many events have a camera team to take photos, by the time you get them (*if* you get them, even when promised), they will be stale for use on social media. Furthermore, the camera team is not focused on *you*, so the pictures may not be usable for your purposes. Ask your friends to take some photos of you:
  - Speaking on the panel.
  - Conversing with a fellow panelist.
  - With ALL of the panelists.

- o   With EACH panelist.
- o   With the panel moderator.
- o   With all of the panelists AND the moderator.
- o   Chatting with audience members after the panel is over.
- o   Anything else that catches their eye, for instance, the use of a prop, an unusual gesture, laughing, etc.
- **TAKE VIDEO.** Unless you are working with a huge audience in a large room with a meeting organizer who has a sizeable budget in the face-to-face world, you will probably *not* have the session recorded. Of course, if it is done remotely, you should get access to the recording. Have your friends get some video footage of you in action. Get a few of these videos and you can put a montage video together that can serve as a demonstration of your expertise as a panelist.
- **POST ON SOCIAL.** Have your friends post during the panel, using the meeting hashtag and joining in the social conversation. You can also inform your friends who cannot attend to follow and share the posts as well.

Here's a quick reference sheet at this QR Code to give your friends so they won't forget to take pictures and video!

CHAPTER THREE
COUNTDOWN TO SHOWTIME!

I love the moment right before a panel discussion begins. There's this nervous energy in the room, and everyone is buzzing with anticipation about what's to come. It's a feeling of excitement mixed with a little bit of fear, and I think it's one of the things that makes live events so special.

Arianna Huffington
Greek-American author & syndicated columnist

Meet-ups and coming early to the panel discussion allow you to familiarize yourself with the environment, network with other attendees, and mentally prepare yourself for the discussion ahead.

This chapter will guide you through what to expect before the panel discussion actually takes place.

DO WE MEET THE OTHER PANELISTS BEFORE THE EVENT?

If the meeting organizer or panel moderator does not initiate a brief call amongst the panelists, suggest a short conference call or video conference a week or two before the panel. Thirty minutes should be sufficient. This "pre-event meet-up" allows the opportunity for everyone to connect, hear the same information sent in the invitation, ask any format questions, and ensure the panelist content is not going to overlap.

This time will be used to discuss the content in general terms, NOT conducting the panel beforehand!

Here are some key items that typically get covered during the pre-event call:

- **WELCOME.** The meeting organizer and/or the panel moderator gives opening remarks
- **PANEL INFO.** Panel title and objectives.
- **SELF-INTRODUCTIONS.** Name and two-sentence focus area of expertise, approach, or opinion.
- **AUDIENCE.** Review the audience demographics and size.
- **PANEL FORMAT.** Review the format/agenda.
- **QUESTIONS.** Sharing of questions the moderator may ask and soliciting questions the panelists envision to be asked and/or have prepared to answer.
    - This is a great time to share the key messages you want to communicate, allowing for some flexibility if another panelist wants to briefly touch on your subject area.
    - If there IS another panelist with some potential overlaps, take a quick moment to confirm that the panelist is not duplicating what you are saying or schedule a separate time to chat.
- **VISUALS.** Will props, slides, or other items be allowed to help the conversation or illustrate a key point?
- **OTHER?** Open the floor for any questions from the panelists.
- **EVENT MEET UP.** Confirm the time and location to meet 30-60 minutes before the event to go over last-minute issues.

During the call, take notes along with the subjects each panelist has agreed to take on. It is a nice touch to email the moderator your notes, and if appropriate, suggest they email the notes to all panelists.

This pre-event call is a great opportunity to establish a working relationship with the other panelists and it is good networking for you too. It is also a nice touch to connect with them on LinkedIn or other appropriate social media platforms.

It is also not uncommon for the meeting organizer to invite the panel to go to breakfast, lunch, or dinner together on the day of the panel. This is meant to be an opportunity to relax, get to know each other, and build a rapport that will be helpful on stage. Again, it is *not* the place to hold the panel discussion.

HOW CAN I CALM MY NERVES?

A little worried or nervous about your upcoming panel discussion? Here is the good news: Stage fright or presentation anxiety is fairly common for new panelists, manifesting itself with dry mouth, sweaty palms, and an increased heart rate.

Here is even better news: there are specific techniques you can use to reduce anxiety, and here are twenty ways to calm your nerves before a panel discussion.

1. **CHAT WITH THE MEETING ORGANIZER.** The meeting organizer has sent you an invitation with all the details and/or set up a call to go over the details. This is a good time to ask any questions that might be keeping you up at night. As you get closer to the date, you can always pick up the phone or send an email to ask about any of those "what ifs" you have rattling around in your brain.

2. **CHECK OUT YOUR FELLOW PANELISTS.** Google their work and the views they hold on the topic. As you review their social footprint (websites, social profiles, book reviews, bios, blogs, recent presentations, media mentions, papers, etc.), note where you have similar and different points of view.

3. **KNOW YOUR AUDIENCE.** Find out who will be in your audience and think about what they need to know about the topic. As you do this, you will become more familiar with them and their expectations.

4. **KNOW THE FIRST QUESTION.** Ask the panel moderator how they will introduce you and what the first question will be. Knowing how it will start and your first interaction will make the transition into the panel easier.

5. **PRACTICE YOUR KEY MESSAGES.** Unlike giving a presentation, you cannot practice your speech, but you can practice your three key messages along with an example, a story, demonstration, or prop that will make your idea come to life as well as a short, memorable headline.

6. **PREPARE A LIST OF POTENTIAL QUESTIONS.** The panel moderator might have shared the questions, but maybe not. Think about what questions the moderator and/or audience might ask about the topic in general and what specific questions they might ask *you* about the topic. Then prepare clear and succinct answers to those questions.

7. **PREPARE "I DON'T KNOW" RESPONSES.** One of your fears may be that you are caught flat-footed and unable to answer the question. For those questions you are not sure about, have a few different responses in your back pocket.

8. **USE NOTES.** Have your key messages on some index cards or your phone, especially if you have some statistics or hard-to-remember examples. You may not even need them, but you will have them handy if you need them.

9. **GET A GOOD NIGHT'S SLEEP.** Go to bed at a normal time and do not worry about the panel. I know, easier said than done. You were asked to share your experience and your perspective, so no need to fret. You will be awesome!

10. **ARRIVE EARLY.** Show up with plenty of time so you feel calm vs. rushed and frazzled. When you arrive, seek out the meeting organizer, the panel moderator, and other panelists.

11. **MINGLE.** Warm up your vocal cords by chatting with colleagues or audience members. Find out something interesting about them. Now you will have some friends in the room.

12. **BE AUTHENTIC.** Be true to your natural style and allow your unique personality to shine.

13. **SMILE.** We know that smiling releases endorphins, which help to calm your nerves, especially when you smile at that friend you just made.

14. **CHECK OUT THE ROOM.** Take a peek into the room where the panel discussion will be. Envision yourself having a great discussion that delivers fabulous value to the audience.

15. **BREATHE.** Sounds obvious, but take a few deep breaths to calm your nervous system. David Greenberg, author of the book *Simply Speaking* recommends that you say to yourself "I am" as you inhale and "relaxed" as you exhale.

16. **STAY HYDRATED.** Prevent anxiety-induced cotton mouth by drinking plenty of water before the panel. Do not forget to go to the bathroom before starting. Make sure there is a bottle of water near your chair.

17. **LISTEN TO MUSIC.** Put your earbuds in and listen to your favorite song.

18. **MEDITATE BRIEFLY.** Find a quiet place, even a toilet stall, and close your eyes to block out distractions. Focus on your breathing. As thoughts arise in your mind, acknowledge them and let them go, allowing your breathing to become slower and deeper.

19. **MOVE.** Moving your body and getting your heart pumping also releases endorphins. Exercise in the morning, take a brisk walk around the conference center, or stretch your muscles to calm your nerves in a jiffy.

20. **AVOID CAFFEINE.** Coffee can make your throat scratchy and other caffeinated drinks can make you jittery and increase your heart rate. Not a good look so just do not drink it.

21. **LEARN THE ART OF STATE SHIFTING.** Adam Guild in Forbes says, "Fixing nervousness before a big pitch or meeting [or panel discussion] requires a state shift. This is a switch in your mind and emotions. When you're worried about what others will think of your pitch, you're probably in your head and in a people-pleasing mode. Instead of hoping they like you and your presentation, focus on them, on the value you're bringing and how it will improve their lives."

SHOULD I USE A MICROPHONE?

If you are on a panel with more than 50 people in the audience, chances are you will need to use a microphone during a panel discussion. If there is a microphone, use it. Even if you think you have a booming voice, it gets tiresome for the audience and is odd if you opt-out.

Here are some general tips on using a microphone during a panel discussion.

- **CHECK WITH A/V TECHNICIANS.** Before the panel, touch base with your A/V technicians. Are they just setting up the system and then leaving the room or will there be a technician be available for the duration?
- **KNOW WHAT IS ON/OFF.** Make sure you know how to turn your microphone/pack on and off, or if the A/V techs are going to do it. We often assume the microphone is "off" when we get it, but it may actually be "on" and then we end up turning it "off".
- **NEW BATTERIES.** Ask if the microphone has new batteries. If not, nicely ask them to put fresh ones in the microphone. You do not want to lose power in the middle of the panel. P.S. I always bring fresh batteries with me, just in case, as I have had to search high and low for batteries.
- **SOUND CHECK.** Have the A/V tech adjust the sound levels for your voice. If you are going to be moving about the room, walk around and see if there are any points of feedback, usually close to the loudspeakers or dead spots to stay away from.
- **NO TAPPING.** Do not tap or blow into the microphone to see if it is turned on. Expert MC Timothy Hyde says, "Microphones have a fairly sensitive diaphragm inside that collects up the sound and then converts it into electrical signals—and you can damage the microphone by blowing into it or tapping it. An alternative is to snap your fingers just in front or run your fingernail lightly across the top which will tell you if it is on or not."

- **TURN OFF YOUR CELLPHONE.** Some microphones pick up the tiny signal a phone makes periodically as it checks into the network. Be extra safe and turn your phone "off" or on "airplane mode" (not just silenced) for the duration of the panel.
- **ASSUME IT IS LIVE.** You do not want to be *that* person who says something between friends and finds out it has been broadcasted throughout the room. Always assume the microphone is "on", live, and broadcasting.

But wait! This list of tips to use a microphone during a panel discussion gets even better as there are some nuances you need to know regarding each of your most typical microphone options:

TIPS FOR USING A LAVALIER

- **LOCATION TO CLIP.** A lavaliere microphone has a small microphone with a wire that connects to the transmitter. The microphone typically has a small alligator clip that attaches to your clothing, somewhere. For men, that typically is the jacket or tie. For women, well, you need to think that through as you want to be able to clip it within two fists of your mouth. Do not forget about clipping the transmitter, typically on your belt. If you do not have a belt, you will want to think that through too.
- **QUIET JEWELRY.** Especially for women when using a lavaliere microphone, think about your jewelry. Does it move, clank, and/or clatter when you move? Those noises will be terribly distracting.
- **BATHROOM BREAK.** Make sure your microphone is "off" or disconnect the microphone from the transmitter before you take a bathroom break. You do not want the audience to hear you tinkling!

TIPS FOR USING A HANDHELD

- **DISTANCE TO YOUR MOUTH.** As a general rule, hold the microphone about a fist or two away from your mouth. Closer and you will hear too many gurgles and pops. Too far away and why bother using a microphone?
- **HOLD DELICATELY.** Expert MC Timothy Hyde says, "Don't hold the microphone in a death grip or wrap your hand around the bottom half of the capsule like a rapper! With cheaper microphones, your hand grip around the barrel creates extraneous noise."
- **BE DYNAMIC.** You can use a handheld microphone to lean in to tell a secret, use a deeper voice to accentuate a key point and create more energy in your words.

TIPS FOR USING A STAND MIC

- **IN/OUT.** Make sure you know how to get the microphone easily in/out of the stand if needed.
- **UP/DOWN.** Also know how to raise/lower the microphone stand, if needed.
- **SHARING.** If you are going to be sharing the microphone on a stand between panelists, agree on how to "pass the microphone" between your fellow panelists.

TIPS FOR USING A LECTERN

- **STAND UP STRAIGHT.** These are very sensitive microphones. Adjust the height to be the same height as your mouth. Stand up straight and talk like a normal person. You do not need to lean into the microphone.
- **LIMIT PAPER.** You may want to have some notes, but keep it simple as the microphone is so sensitive, it will even pick up the rustling of your paper.

Of course, there are other microphone options such as the headset microphone, a corded (or line) handheld microphone, or even a throwable microphone, but those are more the exceptions than the norm.

SHOULD I BRING MY NOTES ON STAGE?

Of course you can! For new panelists or veterans, bringing your notes on stage is typically a matter of preference.

There are four different options to consider:

1. **NO NOTES.** Frankly, I do not suggest this for inexperienced panelists, but if you got the goods, and you are capable and confident, go for it!
2. **ONE SHEET.** You have done enough work that you just need a little confidence to be able to glance at your notes to remind yourself of a key message, story, statistics, etc.
3. **DETAILED SCRIPT.** Perhaps it is your first time and you WANT to bring all your preparation up to the stage with you. If that will make you more comfortable and confident, why not? Once you get into the panel discussion, you may not need all that information.

4. **SOMEWHERE IN BETWEEN.** During your prep work and practice, you will naturally be more comfortable and confident with some portions than others. Just print out the pieces you think you will need some helpful reminders.

Additionally, there are five different methods to bring your notes on stage with you:
1. **PAPER.** The easiest (and most obvious) way to bring your notes with you on stage is to print it out on sturdy, durable paper. 20lb paper is a bit too flimsy, while card stock is a bit too rigid.
2. **LAMINATE.** If you are only using one sheet of paper (one side or both), why not laminate it or put it in a plastic protector? Spilled beverages can happen too!
3. **INDEX CARDS.** Print each point on a separate index card and punch a hole in the upper left corner. Keep them together with a small ring so you can turn the cards easily and they will not fall out of order.
4. **TABLET.** Forget the paper and do the same thing on your tablet. The nice thing about using a tablet is that it does not matter how big or small your notes are.
5. **TELEPROMPTER.** Just like a TV newscaster, upload your notes to a teleprompter. This is typically a "high-end" broadcast option to open and close important panel discussions. Yet, it could get in the way during the actual "discussion" part of the panel.

Finally, here are five tips to make your notes worth looking at:
1. **CREATE EYE DRAMA.** Because you are massively multitasking (listening to the panelists, determining what you will do/say next, AND trying to glance at your notes), create a little drama on the paper/screen to attract the eye. Bold, highlight, or underline some of the text. Use color to differentiate segments. Asterisks or stars for things you cannot forget.
2. **BRING A PEN.** You might want to make some notes, so leave some white space and margins to write in.
3. **GO BIG!** Print or view the text in a sans serif font at least 14-point with 1.5 line spacing, more if you wear glasses and do not want to have to wear them on stage.
4. **STAPLE IT.** Do not forget to staple multiple pages and put the page numbers in a large font on the top right of the page. Collisions can also happen.
5. **USE A CLIPBOARD.** My favorite way to bring notes on stage with me is to use a white leather clipboard to keep the papers looking a tad bit more

professional. A clipboard also provides a hard surface to scribble some notes on.

Whatever you decide, be intentional about your choice. Use the notes while you practice, and you may discover that you do not need notes after all!

HOW EARLY SHOULD I GET TO THE VENUE?

Show up on time, which means whenever the panel moderator asked you to show up. There might be a quick meet-up in the meeting room or green room, or you are getting together over breakfast, lunch, or dinner. Either way, plan on arriving a little earlier as Murphy's Law rules—anything that can go wrong, will go wrong.

I like to get to the venue an hour or so earlier than the panel's start time for several reasons:

- **THE EVENT.** Listen in on the opening keynotes and speakers to get a sense of the overall vibe of the event.
- **THE VENUE.** Make sure you ask the meeting organizer/panel moderator if you can get access to the meeting room ahead of time. Not only can you check out the location, seating arrangements, and how to walk on and off the stage, but you can practice a few lines to get a feel for room acoustics and ambiance. Check out the panelists' chairs and sit up and down repeatedly. This may sound a bit dorky, but most people who spend a lot of time at their desks show the top of their heads. Get out of your seat with your head up, looking at the audience.
- **THE MODERATOR.** Let the moderator know you arrived and find out if there is anything new you need to know.
- **THE PANELISTS.** This is a great opportunity to meet your fellow panelists before things start up. While some panelists will want to start talking about the topic, try not to! Save that organic, authentic, and stimulating conversation for the panel.
- **YOUR NOTES.** Take a moment to review your notes and key talking points.
- **YOUR FRIENDS.** Catch up with the colleagues you asked to join you.
- **THE AUDIENCE.** Chat with as many friendly faces as you can. Casually listen in on their conversations to get a sense of the mood in the room. Introduce yourself; Shake people's hands; Thank them for coming; Get to know their names; Ask them easy questions, such as, "What brings you here today?" or "What's your name and where do you hail from?"

Dig deeper and try, "What's your biggest challenge relating to [the topic]?" You are not only establishing rapport with the audience but also gathering valuable information *about them* that you can incorporate into the discussion.

When you get to the event early, you will feel much more relaxed and in tune with what is about to happen.

CHAPTER FOUR
ANSWER QUESTIONS

The key to answering questions in a panel discussion is to provide valuable insights that add to the conversation rather than just restating what has already been said.

Sheryl Sandberg
American technology executive, philanthropist & writer

Other than introductory remarks or presentations, the bulk of a panel discussion centers around the moderator or the audience asking questions to the panelists.

Q&A is often the biggest fear for many panelists. What if I get asked a hard-ball question? What if I cannot answer it? What if I do not get any questions at all? This chapter is full of ideas and starter sentences to handle questions tactfully and gracefully.

HOW DOES A TYPICAL Q&A SESSION RUN?

At some point during a panel discussion, the panel moderator will turn to the audience and ask for questions. Most folks call this **Audience Q&A** where the moderator takes questions from the audience via text, app, question card, open microphone, or Oprah-style, depending on the event.

To facilitate a meaningful Q&A session, a powerful panel moderator will:
- **DESCRIBE THE PROCESS.** The moderator will share the process they will use to solicit questions e.g. text, app, question card, open microphone, use of microphone runners, or wander into the audience.
- **REVIEW THE GROUND RULES.** The moderator will share any specifics about how they want the Q&A session to run. For example, a moderator may say,

"Please stand, state your name and organization, the name of the panelist you are directing the question to, your one-sentence question, and a few sentences to clarify your question if necessary. Panelists, please speak to the audience when answering all the questions. Now, what questions do you have?"

- **REPEAT THE QUESTION.** The moderator may repeat, restate or summarize the question for the entire audience to hear and for it to be picked up on any recordings being made. They may also reframe tangential questions to be more on-topic.
- **PROMPT A PANELIST.** When the question is for *anyone* on the panel, the moderator may restate the question and then direct the question to a panelist who:
    - Is signaling to the moderator that they want to answer the question e.g. lean forward, raise your hand subtly, or whatever you agreed to in the pre-meeting.
    - They feel would best answer the question.
    - Has not responded as much as the others.
- **TAKE THE NEXT QUESTION.** If a large number of people raise their hands at the start of the Q&A session, the moderator may start with the first person who raised a hand and establish a "queue" or lineup, letting the audience know who will go next.
- **LAST TWO QUESTIONS.** The moderator typically will warn the audience when the session is drawing to a close and that they have time for one or two more questions.

When a panel moderator lays out the process and follows their ground rules, the panelists will be able to answer the questions comfortably and confidently and the Q&A will be the highlight of the panel discussion.

WHAT IS THE BEST WAY TO ANSWER A QUESTION?

Since the bulk of a panel discussion is centered around the moderator or the audience asking questions, the art of answering questions is a critical skill for any panelist to master.

If you are lucky, the panel moderator will give you the list of potential questions they may ask. You may also do a bit of research on your audience to discern potential questions as well. You can also spend a bit of time pondering the likely questions you will be asked and practicing some "head, heart, and hands" answers.

When you are asked a question, treat each person and his or her inquiry as important. Respond professionally, showing that you truly listened to the questioner and you desire to give the best possible response.

Here is a three-step process for the best way to answer a question:

1. **RESTATE THE QUESTION** using the questioner's name.
    - *Paraphrase.* Restate the question in another way so the questioner will know you understand it accurately. This also gives you a moment to formulate your response and lets you re-present the question for anyone who might not have heard it. Be careful of coming across as condescending or putting words in the questioner's mouth by using such phrasing as "What you mean is …" or "What you're trying to say is …"
    - *Repeat.* If the questioner has summarized the question, repeat the end of his summary or pick out key words within the statement to use as your opening words. When you include this in your comments it gives a bit more credence to the question and the questioner, as well as your answer.
    - *Reframe.* Especially when the question is unfocused or unclear, you may want to reframe the question.
    - *Clarify.* If necessary, ask for clarification or probe deeper into the essence of the question. You can ask the person to define part of the question or give an example to illustrate the question.
    - *Parse It Out.* You may find the question is really multiple questions in the guise of one. In which case, enumerate the different questions, and then answer them in the order that makes sense to you. You may even find the "question" is more of a statement, a suggestion, or an idea. If this is the case, acknowledge the contribution and do not even try to "answer" it.
    - *Be Neutral.* Beware of complimenting the person or the question. Unless you are going to say "good question" to every single question, which will get rather tedious and might not always be true, other questioners will feel like their question was not as good.
    - *Affirm.* Although you do not want to compliment, you should be conscious of and acknowledge the underlying purpose or emotion of the other person's questions. Bring it out into the open with

phrases such as, "I sense that this issue is very important to you. I appreciate you bringing this up."

- *Be Open.* You may not like a particular question. It may be too basic, too obvious, or too technical. But it is not about you; your speech is all about meeting *your audience's* needs, so answer their questions as best you can.

- *Suffer the Silence.* You do not have to answer the question immediately. Two seconds of silence to a panelist feels like an eternity. Two seconds of silence to the audience is a heartbeat and is not even noticeable.

2. **RESPOND TO THE QUESTION.** Deliver the first sentence of your answer to the questioner as you would in a normal conversation. Then break eye contact with the questioner and turn your head and body so that you are now talking straight to the audience. Then offer your thoughtful, prepared, and insightful answer to the audience.

3. **END YOUR ANSWER** by connecting it to your point of view with a memorable headline. When you are delivering your last sentence, make sure that your final sweep finishes with you looking back at the questioner so that you end up where you started.

HOW DO I ANSWER A LAME QUESTION?

Ugh. Sometimes, someone from the audience asks a lame question in a panel discussion. As the panel moderator or a panelist, you have three options:

1. Dismiss the question entirely.
2. You lamely repeat it while trying to make some sense of it in your brain.
3. Reframe the question into a "better" question.

Option number one is not an attractive option as The Buckley School cautions, "No one likes the panelist who responds to a statement with 'Is there a question in there?' You don't do your message, your cause, or yourself any favors when you are dismissive of an audience member or their ideas."

Option number two is not attractive either as it makes *you* look like the lame one.

That leaves us with the best and most attractive option number three: to reframe the question into a *better* question. Here are some ideas about how to respond to a lame question when the question is...

- **UNFOCUSED OR UNCLEAR.** Rephrase the question as close to the questioner's words and intention, but give it a bit more clarity. After you have rephrased it, check for agreement. Then again, if you *really* have absolutely no idea what the person is asking, ask the person to "headline" the question for you.
- **WEAK.** Rather than restating or merely repeating the question, tweak a weak question to make it better than it is. Check with the questioner to make sure that is what was meant.
- **TOO SPECIFIC, DETAILED, OR COMPLEX.** Suggest the questioner talk with the panelist immediately after the session. "That's an interesting question, and perhaps better addressed in depth by Panelist A after the wider Q&A we're doing now."
- **LONG-WINDED.** Firmly but politely remind the questioner to state the question. "What is your question?" "Get to the question, please," or you can be a little brash and ask, "Is there a question in there?" Although you may be a patient person and let the questioner finish his or her thought, chances are the real question is lurking in the last spoken sentence. But then again, there may be MULTIPLE questions buried in there, so you may want to tease them out and answer all of them or just one.
- **A COMMENT.** Do not confuse a question with a comment. While the moderator should quickly intervene and remind the entire audience that, "The panelists will be available for comments at the end," and then move briskly to the next questioner, that may not happen. If the comment is directed at you, simply say, "Thank you for your comment."

The key to responding to a lame question (in fact any question at all) is to be respectful to the person who is asking it and to all the audience members who are listening and can benefit from your answer.

HOW DO I SHIFT THE FOCUS OF THE QUESTION?

Let's say you have been asked a decent question (not a lame one) but you would rather shift the focus and take it in a different direction.

You can quickly answer the question (or not) and then "bridge" the question in another direction.

Here are some sentence starters to help shift the focus of the question:
- "Yes, I think that is/may be an issue, but the real issue is…"
- "The question I am often asked is…"
- "Yes, some people are focused on that, but I'm more interested in…."
- "I expected you would have asked me a different question such as …"
- "Another way to look at this question is…"
- "I've got a different take on this question…."
- "Let's step back and take a look at the bigger picture…"
- "There is a much bigger question here…"
- "Let's ask the question behind the question…"

Using one of these sentence starters is an effective way of taking control of the conversation and highlighting the key messages that will benefit the audience.

WHAT IF I DON'T HAVE ANYTHING TO ADD?

You might find yourself the last in the line to answer the exact same question. You witness the dominoes of ideas falling as each panelist shares their brilliance. In your heart of hearts, you simply KNOW that all your great ideas will already be mentioned by the time the hot potato gets to you.

Gulp. You scratch your head. Your palms get sweaty. What in the world are you going to say?

Do not despair. Even though your main points may have been covered, you still have your own unique examples and memorable headline to share.

Try these sentence starters to expand the conversation and provide more insight into the topic:
- "To build on the great example given by Ravi, I'd like to offer an example of my own…."
- "It appears Ravi and I are on the same wavelength. I'd also like to add to it with some of the evidence based on my own research…."

- "That's a great point, Ravi. Your insights echo my own experience and remind me of a story that…."
- "I agree with Ravi, and there is another strategy that has been vital to our success…"
- "Ravi is right on the money. Now let's dive into how we can actually do that. In my experience…"
- "That's a great idea, Ravi. If anyone in the audience is looking to implement that idea, here's a best practice (or tip) on how to do that."
- "That's such a great point, Ravi, and here's *why* that is so important for this audience to understand."
- "We did the same thing as you, Ravi, but for different reasons…"

If you think about it, you will ALWAYS have something to add to the conversation based on your own unique perspective.

Then again, you can try this novel approach used by Kay Thrace (not her real name). She was the last-in-line during a panel with a bunch of lawyers. She answered with a crazy, funny answer, which ultimately tied to her real point that no one else was making. Here is how it went down:

"I had the honor of sitting on an alumni panel recently where the moderator asked each of us what special skill sets we had developed over our years of our practice. Since I had to go last and all the other good answers had been taken, I replied that I was uniquely qualified to survive a zombie apocalypse. Everybody tittered politely and eventually, I conceded and said, 'You need to be likable.' Again everybody dutifully laughed, but I was being deadly serious. About that and surviving the zombie apocalypse.

Why be likable? Because it's in your best interest and it's amazing how many attorneys I meet who don't bother to master this simple skill that should have been learned back in grade school."

When the audience needs a break from the monotony of the answers, throw in a curve ball. Give a bizarre answer. It will buy you a bit of time before you interject with your best answer, or the moderator will move on, thankful that all the panelists had airtime to answer the question.

WHAT IF I DON'T KNOW THE ANSWER?

One of your fears may be that you are caught flat-footed and unable to answer the question. If you are asked something you are not sure about, have a few different responses in your back pocket, such as:

- "That's a good question, Carlos. I don't have the answer right now, but I'll get back to you on that."
- "My initial view on that is X. It's a good question, Carlos. Let me have the team dig into that this week, and I'll send out a fuller response." Make yourself a note to follow through on your promise.
- If someone else on the panel might be able to answer the question, pass the ball to them by saying, "I have never experienced this myself, but perhaps Carlos has some ideas on this?"
- "Let me turn this back to the audience: Does anyone have thoughts or a view on that right now?"

HOW DO I ANSWER THE "GOTCHA" QUESTION?

Every panelist's worst nightmare is the gotcha question: the panel moderator asks a question out of left field, leaving you staring like a deer in headlights. Modeled by our 24/7 news cycle, interviewers are poised to ask "gotcha questions" that can be clipped into sound bites to travel the world instantaneously, often detached from the context in which it was said. Here are nine different types of "gotcha" questions:

1. **THE LEADING QUESTION** suggests the desired answer.
2. **THE LOADED QUESTION** presupposes an unverified assumption.
3. **THE NEGATIVE QUESTION** is phrased so negatively you feel like you have no room to answer.
4. **THE FAULTY PREMISE** is based on inaccurate information or an assertion that is not true.
5. **THE AMBUSH** is a provocative question asked in an unexpected situation.
6. **THE NON-QUESTION** is a comment or statement vs. an actual question.
7. **THE HYPOTHETICAL QUESTION** is about something that has not actually happened yet.
8. **THE "LEFT-FIELD" QUESTION** has no relationship to the topic or the reason why you are speaking.

9. **THE PERSONAL ATTACK** questions the panelist's character often verging into the unpleasant, personal, and/or possibly offensive realm.

As an expert panelist or during any other interview for that matter, you can proactively prepare for cage-rattling questions, recognize the gotcha question, and reframe your response so that you can come out looking like a champ:

1. **PROACTIVELY PREPARE.**
    - *Research.* Media Relations Expert Jan Fox recommends you research the panel moderator, media host, and panelists. Listen to their podcasts, watch their shows, Google their reviews, check for by-lines, and note any "gotcha" questions they tend to ask.
    - *Reflect.* Clarity Coach and Strategist Pam Leinmiller suggests that you examine your vulnerabilities. Ask yourself, "Who is this audience and what are their biggest concerns? What is their paradigm? Where are they coming from? How will do I anticipate they will respond to my message? Is it controversial, new, or revolutionary?"
    - *Anticipate.* You already have a good sense of where the gotcha questions will come from. Business Book Strategist Cathy Fyock recommends you write down the worst questions you might be asked under whatever circumstance in two minutes. You might be surprised how many questions you can think of. Extend your search by talking to colleagues and those who understand the topic/situation by asking them, "If you wanted to catch me off guard, what would you ask me?"
    - *Practice.* Have someone ask you these tough questions. Fox advises you to "Rehearse short and concise answers, without 'memorizing' the answers. You know your material, so speak answers from what you know. That way you will not get tripped up."
    - *Prepare.* For each point you want to make, have an astounding fact, an interesting three-line story, an analogy, or a comparison to add along with a 15-second sticky, repeatable, and memorable headline or sound bite.

2. **RECOGNIZE THE GOTCHA QUESTION.**
    - *Actively Listen.* When asked a question, listen carefully. Try not to formulate a response to the question while the question is being asked or make an assumption about the questioner.

- *Spot It!* Notice the loaded trigger words containing emotions, assumptions, faulty logic, or hypothetical verbiage.
- *Deeper Meaning.* Listen for the real question behind the question. What is actually prompting the question?
- *Pause.* Take a moment to give yourself time to think about how you can rephrase the question.

3. **RESPOND TO THE REFRAMED QUESTION.** Media Expert Alan Stevens recommends a three-part "neutral rephrasing" to respond to the question:
    - *Clarify the Question.* Use specific language teeing up the fact you are giving focus to the question you are willing to ask such as: "For the benefit of everybody else who might not have caught all of that, let me clarify what you are asking" or "What you want to know is…"
    - *Rephrase.* As you clarify, frame the question in your own neutral, non-judgmental way. Media Training Expert Rosemary Ravinal recommends you "Take the negative and emotional words out of the question and rephrase the question into the answer you already prepared!"
    - *Answer.* Respond to your rephrased question and *not* the gotcha question. Bring it back to the facts and do not respond to the emotional underpinnings of the question. Be concise. Only answer as much as is necessary and move on to the next question.

For multi-part questions, Stevens suggests you start with the question you can answer most confidently and in some detail. Say, "Let me take that second point that you've raised first." Then go back to the questioner and say, "I believe you had some other points." Don't say, "I've forgotten your questions". More often than not, they will nod that your answer was fine.

If you do not know, be transparent and tell the questioner and the audience that you will find out and get back to them in the most appropriate way. Leinmiller says, "Honesty is the best policy. Rather than saying, 'I don't know,' frame your answer positively by starting with 'Here's what I CAN tell you.' Tell them what you know, give a reference for more information if you have one, and move on to the next question.

Even though it appears that *the questioner* has control of Q&A, the savvy, prepared panelist has ultimate command of the conversation. "You're in control of what you say because you already have the answers and the clear intention of what you want to say," Ravinal explains. "While the question can be deceptive or tricky, stay on your topic and give the answers you want to give with great clarity and confidence. It may not always match and that's perfectly okay." It is certainly not worth losing sleep over.

WHAT ABOUT THE LAST QUESTION?

Nick Morgan wrote a fabulous book called *Give Your Speech, Change the World*. The same thing holds with panel discussions. What is the point if you do not want the audience to think, feel, or do something as a result of your time together?

With any luck, the panel moderator will tell you their final question and/or how they intend to close the panel. Be sure to take some time to think about a final takeaway, insight, or idea you want to leave with the audience.

Your panel moderator may ask you for:

- An actionable suggestion or "call to action" - based on what the panel discussed.
- ONE thing you want the audience to think, feel, or do as a result of this discussion.
- An idea that we did not mention that we *should* have....
- What *you* learned on this panel that you did not know before.
- The question you are most often asked after talking about what we just talked about.
- What bugs you the most about this topic?
- The best way to contact you for more information.
- If you had to summarize what we discussed here, what would be your headline? Share one of your key points, or favorite quotes, in a "headline" form—a memorable phrase of five to ten words encapsulating your idea. Encourage your audience to write it down or post on social media to solidify the takeaways.

A word of caution: At this point in the panel, you have done a great job sharing valuable information and insights, and you or the moderator have positioned you and/or your organization appropriately. Do not blow it by being too pushy and promotional right at the end. If they are interested, they will reach out to you.

Finish the panel discussion on a high note with a very clear call to action. It is this "final thought" that creates clear takeaways for the audience and positions you and your company as a resource.

CHAPTER FIVE
MAKE IT CONVERSATIONAL

When panelists engage with each other and make the discussion conversational, the audience is more likely to be engaged and interested in what is being said.

Carla Harris
Vice Chairman of Wealth Management at Morgan Stanley

A panel is a discussion and not a dissertation, which means you have to put aside all those structured and stilted panel presentations you have seen and buy into the idea to have a natural conversation between engaged panelists.

Hopefully, you have a meeting organizer and panel moderator who are also aligned with this thinking. Listen for their pre-planning messages that encourage you to engage, interact, converse, be curious, and challenge each other.

This chapter will give you some guidelines about how you can make the panel discussion interesting and conversational.

WHAT IS A GOOD CONVERSATIONALIST?

Have you heard the apocryphal story of a US senator's wife sitting between President Nixon and Secretary of State Kissinger? When asked by a reporter what it was like to sit next to two of the most powerful men in the world, she responded, "Indeed, I was impressed with President Nixon. He shared some wonderfully interesting stories, yet Secretary Kissinger made me feel like *I* was the most interesting person in the room."

Just like an amazing dinner party, you want to be *interested* as well as *interesting*. Here are a few ideas to create a lively and candid conversation among the panelists and with the audience:

- **BE THE BEST VERSION OF YOU**
    - *Actively Listen.* It is easy to sit passively, waiting for your turn to show off your knowledge; however, if you are not listening carefully, you could miss key opportunities to ask follow-up questions or add to your fellow panelists' insights. As they are talking, listen deeply so you will be able to respond accurately and intelligently.
    - *Be Present.* You could also start thinking about all the things you have to do when you get back to the office. NO, do not go there! The most important thing for you to do right now is to be completely present in the moment.
    - *Smile.* Do not forget to tell your face to smile and be friendly. ☺ Even though you are not speaking, the audience will still be looking at you. Stay poised and professional. Use your eyes to show interest, empathy, and understanding.
    - *Bring Energy.* Hopefully, you got a good night's sleep and you are bringing your "A" game to the panel. Sit up straight. Show your enthusiasm for the subject. Stay engaged throughout the entire panel.
    - *Be Honest and Straightforward.* Much of business and life is a struggle and most of us do *not* have it all figured out. Best practices and lessons learned are forged from the crucible of struggle. Be willing to talk honestly about how you overcame your struggles. Share what worked and what did not work along with real-life, concise examples.
- **WHEN YOU ARE TALKING**
    - *Keep the Audience in Mind.* Before you open your mouth, run your idea through the filter of "What is useful to the audience?" rather than saying what you want to talk about or trying to make yourself look good.
    - *Acknowledge Others' Expertise.* Let your fellow panelists know that you took the time to learn about them and their work. For example, "Keisha, I was reading your blog last week and thought your point about that was right on the mark."
    - *Use Conversational Words.* Consider the panel to be a dinner party; not a dissertation. Talk like a human being with words the audience uses every day. Do not try to sound "smart" just because you are the expert. Someone smarter than you could be on the panel or in the audience.

- *Keep it Short.* People prefer snappy, well-thought-out answers to interesting questions. No more than 90 seconds and then "pass the ball."
- *Pass the Ball.* When done speaking, ask another panelist to chime in, pass it back to the moderator or get the audience involved.
- *Watch Your Airtime.* While you should get your fair share of airtime, you do not need to answer every question. Be aware of how many times you have spoken as compared to your fellow panelists and give others a chance to weigh in.
- *Know Your Second.* Which of your fellow panelists can you turn to for help? Which are your allies? Who will support your position? In other words, who will "second" your motion? Turn to your "second," establish eye contact and put them on the spot to offer support: "Keisha, did you have a similar experience?"
- *Piggy Back.* Pick up an interesting bit from another panelist and add to the idea. Remember, be additive and not repetitive. Brainstorm in the moment and bounce ideas off each other—Audiences love the unplanned spontaneity of the conversation!
- *Link Ideas.* Quickly paraphrase and/or comment on a thread of ideas or differences of opinions along with your point of view. For example, "In revealing their struggles, Indira and Sean were highlighting the importance of…"
- *Disagree Respectfully.* Yes, disagreements are common, otherwise, we would have a fairly boring panel. Just do not disagree simply because you can. Disagree because the discussion will benefit the audience *and* your reputation.

- **WHEN OTHERS ARE TALKING**
  - *Be Respectful.* Actively listen to your fellow panelists. Let your colleagues finish their sentences.
  - *Take Notes.* As they are talking, jot down a quick note to be able to refer to a specific comment.
  - *Move Your Head.* Nod your head up and down when you agree with another panelist. When in disagreement, cock your neck to the side to show curiosity about what was just said rather than nod your head side-to-side.

On the other side of the coin, here are a few conversation killers:

- **REPETITION.** If you agree with what is being said, either *expand* on what has been said, *add* new information, or *say nothing*. If asked, say you do not have anything to add.
- **GENERALIZATIONS.** Lofty answers to the questions lack specifics on what the audience can *do* with the information.
- **FIREHOSE.** Especially in academic, engineering, and science panels, panelists can get too focused on sharing *all* the knowledge they know about their life's work. It is just too much to talk about in a short time. Rather than walking away with three concrete ideas, the audience has been packed with more information than a human can consume in one seating. Can you say, "Overload?"
- **LENGTH.** When speaking on a panel, keep it short. No five-minute stories are allowed.
- **CURMUDGEON.** Mind your manners. Do not cut off or interrupt the other panelists or the moderator. Do not disagree just because you are ornery. Avoid sighing, eye-rolling, crossing and uncrossing your legs, shuffling papers, or fiddling with your smartphone.
- **PANEL HOG.** Especially when you know all the answers to the questions the panel moderator is asking, you can be tempted to keep chiming in. Share the spotlight evenly with the moderator and your fellow panelists.
- **PERSONAL ATTACK.** Personal attacks on someone's character, skills, or abilities are a clear line you do not want to cross…ever.

One final note: A good panel moderator will break eye contact with you, forcing you to look away and toward the audience. Expect it and do not feel uncomfortable when this happens to you.

HOW DO I SPARK CONVERSATION?

What do you do when a panel discussion becomes completely dull and lifeless? The energy in the room is flat. Even YOU are semi-bored, and you cannot even rely on the panel moderator to make it lively.

You do *not* need to wait for the panel moderator to add life to a dull panel, nor do you need to ask for permission. You did a fair amount of preparation (see Chapter Two), and you can use that knowledge to your advantage to spark conversation:

- **ASK A QUESTION.**
  - *Ask an Open-Ended Question.* Panelists can ask open-ended questions to the other panelists or the audience to encourage discussion. These questions should be broad enough to allow for a variety of responses and not elicit a simple "yes" or "no" answer.
  - *Ask a Provocative Question.* "Juanita, I'm curious about your views on this topic. In my research for this panel, I discovered that you have a unique take on this. Would you tell us more?"
  - *Pull Out a "Back Pocket" Question.* "What I expected you would ask…"
  - *Ask the Audience a Question.* Take a poll, request more information, or ask a simple question related to the topic.
  - *Ask Yourself a Question.* Have a little fun by raising your hand and asking for permission to ask a question! Go into a serious character/voice and say, "[Your Name], I have a question for you." You then perk up and gleefully say, "Fire away!" Then ask yourself a relevant and interesting question that you already prepared an answer for—and then answer it.
- **SHARE A PERSONAL EXPERIENCE.** Add depth to the conversation and provide a unique perspective by sharing a personal experience. This can also encourage other panelists to share their own experiences and lead to a livelier discussion.
- **CHALLENGE AN ASSUMPTION.** Panelists can challenge assumptions made by other panelists or the audience, which can lead to a deeper exploration of the topic. This can be done respectfully and without being confrontational.
- **BRING UP A RELEVANT EXAMPLE.** Panelists can bring up relevant examples illustrating their points and can help to make the conversation more concrete. These examples can be drawn from their own experiences or current events.
- **SUMMARIZE AND REFRAME.** Panelists can summarize what has been said so far and reframe the conversation, further encouraging discussion. This can be a useful technique if the conversation has become unfocused or if the panelists are talking past each other.
- **LET'S PLAY A GAME.** Pose a quick challenge to the panelists. For example, "Each of you has 30 seconds to describe…" Or play "Would You Rather?" where the panelists are given two options. They choose one and tell the audience why.

- **UNPLANNED SPONTANEITY.** You can also be truly spontaneous in the moment, which is always a surprise for the moderator, fellow panelists, and the audience. The ability to pull this off is largely dependent on the panelist's personal style and confidence. Whatever you do, it has to be interesting *and* benefit the audience. If it works, run with it! If it bombs (which it might), simply move on. No harm, no foul.

Overall, the key to sparking conversation as a panelist is to be engaged and present in the discussion. By actively listening and contributing to the conversation in meaningful ways, panelists can help to create a dynamic and engaging discussion, keeping the audience interested and informed.

HOW DO I ENGAGE THE AUDIENCE?

Don't you get annoyed when panelists solely talk to the panel moderator and their fellow panelists, never addressing the audience? After all, it is the audience that is benefitting from the panel's wisdom. We know from research and practical experience that audience engagement fosters a positive effect, retention of information, and better recall later. Why not engage with the audience directly?

You may not be the panel moderator, but you still can involve the audience in small ways:

- **PREPARE FOR THE PANEL** with the audience in mind. What questions do they want to be answered? What key ideas do you want to convey to them?
- **MINGLE.** Right before the panel starts, introduce yourself to others in the audience. Shake their hands. Thank them for coming. Ask them easy questions so you have some new friends in the audience.
- **EYE CONTACT.** When answering a question or contributing content, direct your answers to the audience, not to the moderator.
- **USE INCLUSIVE LANGUAGE.** Pull the audience in by saying "you" while looking directly into the audience. Use phrases representing them, their interests, and their concerns such as:
  - "Like many in the audience, I…"
  - "We all have…"
  - "Who among us has or hasn't…"
- **BODY POSITION.** Look at how you are sitting. Are you sitting closely with your fellow panelists creating tight conversations or can you shift

your body and be more open to the audience? This positioning can show them that you are aware of and interested in them.

- **AVOID JARGON, ACRONYMS, OR INSTITUTIONAL LANGUAGE.** Just because *you* know what something means does not necessarily mean *they* will. Choose words and terms the audience will understand. You can also pause and provide a parenthetical definition of the term and continue your story.

- **USE STORIES AND EXAMPLES.** Have a story for each key idea, especially if the concept will be new or unfamiliar to the audience.

- **SHOUT OUT.** Perhaps a subject matter expert (SME) is in the room who deserves a mention from the stage. Point to them and ask them to wave their hand or to stand up.

- **CALL ON A PERSON IN THE AUDIENCE.** Call on an audience member to answer a question, comment on what has been said, or ask you a question. For example, you can call on the SME to stand up and offer a different opinion or comment on the subject.

- **POSE A STATEMENT.** Try posing a statement and asking the audience if it is true or false (fact or fiction) or if they agree/disagree.

- **DO SOMETHING.** You can ask them to "Write this down….[important point/headline]" "Applaud if you like vanilla ice cream." Or "Stand up if you are committed to making ice cream available all summer long!"

- **FILL IN THE BLANK.** Ask the audience to complete a sentence or shout out an answer. For example, if the topic is about "disruption," ask the audience to shout out their definition of "disruption."

- **TAKE AN INFORMAL POLL.** If you do not know the cast of characters in the room or want to gauge the level of interest, take a quick, informal poll of the audience.

- **VERBAL RESPONSE.** Preachers do this all the time: If you believe you are going to heaven, say, "Amen!" and the audience shouts "Amen!" You could also tell the audience to say, "Hallelujah," exclaim "Oh Yeah!" or shout out "Uh-huh!" If confidentiality is important, ask for those to agree to hum. You will find those who are passionate will hum loudly! You can also ask the audience to say, "Oh no," shout out "No way," or even "Boo" if they do not agree. The volume of the response can also show the strength of the audience's interest level and/or commitment.

- **NUDGE YOUR NEIGHBOR.** Ask a provocative question and ask the audience to talk about it for a minute with their neighbor(s). People will automatically gravitate to groups of two or three no matter the size of the audience.

- **ENJOY Q&A.** Some panelists dread Q&A, fearing bad questions or being put on the spot. You can prepare for these potentially pesky moments by checking out Chapter Four, which helps if you approach Q&A as an opportunity to learn from the audience as well.
- **CREATE A CALL TO ACTION.** A conversation can be robust and scintillating, but if you do not ask the audience to do anything with what they have heard, it is just that. Great conversation, but no real ramifications. Why not make a request?

As a general rule to engage the audience more, consider the audience as the final panelist so you do not forget about them in the conversation. Look at them and engage with them, just like you would with your fellow panelists.

HOW TO TAKE A QUICK, IMPROMPTU POLL

1. **TURN TO THE AUDIENCE.** Look directly at the audience and turn your body as much as you can to "address" them.
2. **ASK THE QUESTION AND MODEL THE BEHAVIOR.** Do what you want to see. For example, "Who here…." and while you are asking the question, raise your hand high in the air. This sends a clear signal that you are expecting those in the audience who will say "yes" to follow your behavior.
3. **REPORT THE RESULT.** You may be the only person in the room who can see all the results, and inquiring minds want to know. Share the results in the form of a statistic: "That looks like thirty folks, so that's 10 percent of the group."

   Want to make it a tad bit funny? Report out the numbers in a precise way, even though it is obviously your best guesstimate. For example, you could say "Twenty-seven folks agree, and that is 13.3 percent of the group.")
4. **FOLLOW UP.** You can zoom in on a couple of people near you and ask them some additional questions to get the conversation going. If the poll turns out to be heavily weighted in one direction, then turn to your fellow panelists and ask them for a reason why the audience is wrong. For example, if you ask the audience, "How many of you believe salespeople are dishonest?" and 80 percent of the audience agrees, turn to a panelist and ask, "Give me one reason they're wrong."

Note: A quick poll requires one choice and one action, which you believe the majority of the people in the audience will be in agreement. Equally as important is the behavior/response/activity that they will actually *do*. People will say "Hallelujah" or "Praise the Lord" in a church, but will they willingly and loudly say it in front of their peers? Only you can decide.

By including interaction, however small, the audience has an active role and is less inclined to become bored or distracted.

SHOULD I USE FIRST NAMES OR TITLES?

Legendary American author and speaker Dale Carnegie once said, "Remember that a person's name is to that person the sweetest and most important sound in any language."

Everyone loves to hear his or her name, especially during a panel discussion. It makes them feel heard, noticed, and special.

Just listen to the difference as you read these two sentences aloud:

> "That's an insightful question, Carlos. I'd like to offer an alternative perspective"

> "That's an insightful question and I'd like to offer an alternative perspective."

When you use a person's name, it acknowledges their contribution. In addition, whenever you hear your name, a happy chemical is released inside your brain!

Dr. John B. Molidor, CSP, CEO and President of Brain Based Leadership Institute explains, "To understand one event, it is important to note that from the moment you were born, your brain is looking for 'wiring' instructions. At birth and into your youth, these instructions came from your parents and/or caregivers.

As your name is repeatedly called, your brain wires it in place and it is stored in memory. As you get older, two other neurochemicals come into play—dopamine and serotonin. Dopamine is the so-called 'feel-good' chemical and serotonin is a 'contentment' chemical. Thus, when you hear your name, your brain compares it to your stored memory and releases dopamine and serotonin. You feel good and you feel content…Using another's name is a positive way to make a connection with that person."

To use people's names, you have to *remember* their names! The moderator may have name tents but you probably will not be able to see them. They are there more for the audience than for the panelists. Do not worry! Here are a few tips on remembering the moderator and panelist names:

- In your prep work, look at the program or LinkedIn profiles to match the name with their pictures.
- Write down their names in the order they are sitting on your clipboard or tablet.
- In the virtual world, write the names down on a sticky note and place it above eye level on your monitor so you can refer to it.

Make it a habit of using people's names. Consider using official titles for formal panels and first names for more informal panels. Be sure to pronounce the names correctly.

Quick Note: Whether you use first names or official titles, be consistent using the same format for ALL the panelists. You do not want to be accused of an unconscious bias (e.g. calling all the female panelists by their first names and male panelists by their official titles).

Lastly, if you have a personal preference about how you want to be addressed, be sure to tell the panel moderator.

HOW DO I INSERT MYSELF IN THE DISCUSSION?

As a panelist, you may not be able to insert yourself into a panel discussion. Perhaps it is because you are an introvert, you are sitting at the end of a long row of panelists, you are the outsider and all the other panelists know each other well, or simply no one has asked you to comment.

Regardless of the cause, the moderator is not balancing the airtime and you simply cannot get a word in edgewise. Not to worry. Here are some easy things to do to insert yourself into a panel discussion:

- **SHIFT YOUR MINDSET.** Screenwriter and producer Patrick Allan says, "If you feel like you struggle to be heard, there is a good chance that a lot of it comes from your own mind. You might think it is important for you to sound intelligent or funny...Change your perspective on the whole ordeal." Again, think casual dinner party with friends where everyone should have a chance to talk. Allan continues with a pool metaphor: "It's a pool full of splashing kids, having a good time, so take off the floaties and dive in!"

- **APPRECIATE YOUR ROLE.** Perhaps you are intimidated by the other panelists and are hesitant to barge into the conversation. Do not forget that you were asked to provide a specific perspective on the topic, and you are depriving the audience of your knowledge. Make sure you come prepared with your three talking points with concise, corresponding stories.

- **ADJUST YOUR BODY.** Take a look in the mirror. Your natural stance may be sending subliminal signals that you *do not* want to talk. Crossed arms, looking at your notes, fidgeting, etc. can lead the moderator to direct the conversation to others. Lea McLeod at The Muse recommends "A neutral pose that shows you are engaged, but not presumptuous. Use open body language (i.e., do not cross your arms), avoid extreme facial expressions (regardless of whether they are favorable or disapproving), and nix the foot tapping and other fidgety habits that signal impatience."

- **LISTEN ACTIVELY.** If there are four panelists, each person will only be able to talk 25% of the time, so you will be in listening mode the majority of the time. Keep eye contact, nod when you agree, and react appropriately to what is being said. David Morin says, "As long as you are involved in what is being said and show it with your body language, people will see you as part of the conversation even if you actually do not say much." The added benefit of being a good listener is that they will direct their attention to you when you speak.

- **SIGNAL THE MODERATOR.** One of the main roles of a panel moderator is to balance the airtime evenly between panelists. They should be constantly scanning the panelists and creating space for them to weigh in as appropriate. When ready to speak, look directly at the moderator, lean in, and open your hands as if you are going to say something. A savvy moderator will create a space for you to break into the conversation.

- **DIVE IN!** When you have something to say, do not wait for an invitation. Seek a small break in the conversation, even if a fellow panelist is just taking a breath. Confidently lower your voice in tone, lean in, open your hands, and share a quick comment about what the panelist just said, add the word "and," and share what you want to say. The gestures trigger people's motion sensing, and everyone's eyes will be drawn toward you. Here are a few useful phrases:

- o "May I add something here?"
- o "I'd like to respond to something Kendrick just said."
- o "I'd like to offer a contrasting view."
- o "Kendrick, we've been overlooking an important point…"
- **INTERRUPT.** Sometimes, the only way to get to speak is to interrupt the moderator or a panelist. This can be easier said than done for most people. Have some "starter" phrases at the ready if you think this may be a problem:
  - o "Hold on just a moment, Kendrick, I appreciate that point…." State his point concisely and *add to* the conversation.
  - o "Kendrick, what an interesting point, and I'd like to add to that."
  - o "You have an interesting point Kendrick, but I have a different perspective that I'd like to share."

Next time you are feeling left out of the panel, try one of these seven tips to insert yourself in a panel discussion.

CAN I BE A GOOD PANELIST IF I AM INTROVERTED?

Of course you can! An introvert can be a GREAT panelist; however the odds are stacked against them. Why? Because the talkative extroverts suck up all the airtime!

So what is an introvert to do to stack the odds in their favor?

To answer this question, I asked my colleague and author of Creating Introvert-Friendly Workplaces, Jennifer B. Kahnweiler, Ph.D, CSP. "Absolutely!" she agreed. "I've run numerous panels with introverts, and they have been fabulous! The interesting thing about introverts is that their sweet spot is in the preparation. Hopefully, the panel moderator will meet with them, ask for and go over potential questions, and share the theme, focus, and structure of the panel. When an introvert is prepared, they can be present in the moment and able to react confidently."

Kahnweiler continued, "The introvert also needs to be prepared to jump into the conversation and that is tough to do as an introvert!" Best case scenario, the moderator is managing the airtime. Regardless, an introvert should not hesitate to weigh in on the discussion. Kahnweiler suggests preparing a few ways to signal interest in joining the conversation such as a hand signal, leaning forward, or simply using the person's name.

Kahnweiler also emphasized "Another introvert strength is they are great listeners. They can pick up on what other panelists are saying and write down an idea of how that point of view is connected to one of their prepared key messages." Because introverts are so introspective, they can really tune in to the heart of the discussion. When they focus on how they can benefit others with their contributions, they will feel less stress and more confident.

"Generally, introverts are thoughtful, reflective, and tend to use fewer words and more concise language. While the extroverts might be taking more quantitative airtime, the introverts may be sharing more memorable takeaways. Think of the EF Hutton commercial where everyone leans in to listen when EF Hutton talks! That's how it is with the well-prepared messages and stories an introvert will share."

It also helps the introvert to get to the venue early and scope out the stage and the chairs. Some introverts might prefer to sit at the end. Depending on their objectives for being on the panel, they might want to sit in the middle!

Finally, Kahnweiller suggested you let your panel moderator know you are prepared and excited about being on the panel - even if you are an introvert! Remember, you were invited because you have something to offer, and those in attendance want to hear what you have to say!

HOW DO I DISAGREE RESPECTFULLY?

Although you have been selected to speak candidly about your perspective, you may be wondering how to disagree respectfully during a panel discussion. Since you have done your research on your fellow panelists and you know you have differing opinions, you can expect disagreements to happen.

Keep in mind that disagreement in a panel discussion is *crucial* for robust conversation. The key is to learn *how* to recognize them and use them to the benefit of the audience.

My good friend and colleague, Barry Banther, CSP, CPAE made an astute observation about where it *originates*. He said, "When people disagree, be curious about whether it is a disagreement in **principle** or **preference**."

What a gift to probe further to discover if the disagreement is about a fundamental principle that is worth pursuing OR a preference that is worthwhile to note but then move on.

Should you disagree about a fundamental principle that you believe is flawed, here are seven tips on how to disagree respectfully during a panel discussion.

1. **BE CLEAR ABOUT THE AREA OF DISAGREEMENT.** Before you open your mouth to disagree, make sure you have been actively listening and clearly understand the point your fellow panelist is making. If unsure, follow up with curiosity, "Let me make sure I understand you correctly" or "What you're saying is … [summarize your understanding of their argument]."

2. **ENSURE IT IS WORTH THE EFFORT AND ENERGY.** Yes, you were asked to bring differing viewpoints and you want the audience to think you are brilliant, but what would happen if you stayed quiet? What would be the consequences of your silence? What would be the consequences of disagreeing? In the big scheme of things, sometimes you cannot be bothered to waste the effort and energy to disagree.

3. **PROVIDE VALUE TO THE AUDIENCE.** Review the promotional/marketing materials ahead of time and listen closely to the panel moderator's opening comments. These two critical pieces set the expectations for the panel discussion and allow you to align your comments to the panel objectives. Katie Azevedo, M.Ed says, "It's not always our place to disagree with someone in group discussions, and knowing this reality is very important. While self-advocacy is a valuable skill and disagreements often lead to constructive solutions, the greater skill is knowing when it's appropriate to speak up."

4. **TIME IT APPROPRIATELY.** Panel discussions move notoriously quickly, and the conversation may have moved on. The conversation can have a friendly banter-ish vibe going on and you can interject even a minute or two later by saying, "I'd like to come back to what Tamika said just a few minutes ago…" You can also save your idea for the closing remarks if you feel that window of opportunity has closed. Be sure to write down your comments so you will not forget them.

5. **ACKNOWLEDGE THE GOOD BITS.** Chances are your colleague said *something* you agree with. Acknowledge at least some part of their perspective before moving into the areas of disagreement. Try some phrases such as:
    o "I really agree with what you said about point a, yet I disagree with point b."
    o "Thank you for your thoughts on point a, but I'm actually thinking…."

- "I see your point about point a; however, I think [new idea] would work better because [new idea]."
- "You can absolutely do it the way Tamika is suggesting. However, another way to approach this is…"
- "I agree with your point about point a, but I have a different view…"
- "I understand where you are coming from, but I see it differently. The reason why is…"
- "I understand what you're saying about point a, but the way I see it is …"
- "Though I agree with what you're saying about point a, it seems to me that…"
- "While I agree with you on point a, have you considered…?"
- "I understand what you're saying about point a. On this other point…"

6. **BE NICE AND PLAY NICE.** If you disagree, no need to go on the offensive and attack their ideas as "wrong" or "bad." Instead, you simply have a different perspective. Use "I" statements to communicate how you feel, what you think, and what you want or need while remaining calm, cool, and collected.

    - Use "buffering words" to soften the blow:
        - "I'm afraid I disagree."
        - "I don't think that's right/completely true."
        - "I think I have a slightly different point of view."
        - "I'm not quite sure I agree with you."
        - "I beg to differ…"
        - "Not necessarily…"
        - "With due respect, I partly disagree with what you are saying…"
        - "That might be true, but in my experience [new idea]."
        - "I'm not sure that's right/completely true."
        - "I'm not sure that's a good idea because [rationale]."
        - "I'm not sure I can agree with that statement."
    - Take the curious approach and ask questions to follow up on what was said:
        - "Interesting. Are you sure that's possible?"

- "Can you tell me why you think that way?"
- "Let's clarify our assumptions here"
- "You seem to be assuming [xyz]. Do I understand you correctly?"
- "Is this always the case? Are there any exceptions?"

o Take the direct approach:
- "I wouldn't say that…"
- "That's not always the case because [rationale]."
- "That idea is not necessarily true because [rationale]."
- "That idea isn't supported by the evidence."
- "I must respectfully disagree …"
- "I understand how your experiences could lead you to this conclusion; however, my research indicates otherwise."
- "You know I respect you as a professional and you've given a lot to this field over the years. We haven't always seen eye-to-eye and that helps keep us both on our toes. Here's how I see this topic."

7. **BE CONCISE.** Since time is of the essence, speak clearly and concisely, refraining from sharing extraneous and/or irrelevant information and data that you would normally share when talking about this with your colleagues back at work.

Conversely, here are some statements you should NOT use when disagreeing with a fellow panelist:

- "My *honest* opinion would be…" This infers that your other statements weren't honest/as honest.
- "I see your point, *but*…" The "but" negates anything you say afterward, so why not say, "I see your point, *and* [new idea]"?
- "I'm *sorry*. I don't agree." What are you sorry for? Speaking your mind? If you're "sorry" to speak up and you don't think it adds value to the conversation, then don't.
- "No, I don't agree with *you*." This gets into personal territory. Instead of saying "you," say "What you just said."
- "I *totally* disagree with what you just said." Hyperbolic adjectives are not your friends. Words such as "totally," "completely," and "really" are unnecessary words to interject your opinion.

- "That's a *horrible* idea." Whoa! Now we are into judgment territory. Are you the final arbiter of the good, bad, and ugly ideas? If so, then go ahead, but don't be surprised if sparks fly!

"Most important, though, regardless of the technique, is the tone of voice", says Presentation coach Lisa B Marshall. "You must take extra care to keep all sarcasm, anger, or frustration out of your tone. That is really hard sometimes, but having a good frame of mind can help."

Finally, your objective in disagreeing with a fellow panelist in a panel discussion is not to prove yourself right or prove the other person wrong. The goal is to articulate and understand each other's views and possibly even find common ground or a synergistic solution or idea that will benefit the audience.

CHAPTER SIX
AFTER THE PANEL IS OVER

Being on a panel is like being on a roller coaster ride.
Once it's over, you're exhilarated and a little dizzy,
and you need time to process what just happened.
You may also feel like you want to go again,
to try to do better the next time around.

Adam Grant
American author

Congratulations! The panel is over and I hope you found the panelist experience enjoyable *and* valuable. Yet the value of a panel discussion is not just in what is said *during* the session, but also in what happens *after* the panel is over.

This chapter will provide ideas to continue the conversation after the panel discussion, reflecting on the insights shared, and improving your panelist skills.

WHAT DO I DO WHEN THE PANEL IS OVER?

Immediately after the panel is done, you will want to hang around for at least an hour after the panel ends for these five reasons:

1. **CHAT WITH AUDIENCE MEMBERS.** Engage one-on-one with those who come up to you and want to explore something you said. Perhaps they have a question that they did not want to ask in front of the entire room. Maybe they want to take a selfie with you. Shola Kaye, keynote speaker and author of *How to Be a DIVA at Public Speaking* says, "These interactions are arguably as important as sitting on the panel itself. When people see you on stage you're viewed as having influence and

authority. Give back by cheering on your interested audience members and encouraging them to keep in touch."

2. **CONNECT WITH THE OTHER PANELISTS.** Congratulate each other for a job well done! Follow up if they said something you are interested in discussing with them at greater length.

3. **THANK THE MODERATOR.** Share a heartfelt thank you for a nice job with some specific feedback on what you thought went well. Leave the pieces you did not like for your own personal critique of the panel or if the moderator pointedly asks you for feedback.

4. **INTERVIEWS WITH MEDIA.** If the media is at the event, you will not want to miss the opportunity for an interview right after the panel.

5. **NETWORKING.** The event may not be over, so why not use your "speaker appearance" as an icebreaker to meet other people at the conference?

But wait! The panel is not really over. You still have work to do:

- **POST ON SOCIAL MEDIA.** Continue the discussion with your followers and/or the event/panel social hashtag. If appropriate, write about your experience or what was said on your blog or podcast. Pose an interesting question to your social outlets to keep the conversation going.

- **FOLLOW UP.** You will probably receive a few emails or even a card thanking you for your insights. Be sure to respond to each thank you and follow up with all those interesting folks you met.

- **SEND A THANK YOU.** Writing and sending a personal thank you letter to the meeting organizer, panel moderator, and fellow panelists is a polite and lovely touch. In today's world, you may be the only one they receive, and it will set up apart.

- **CONNECT ON SOCIAL MEDIA.** If you have not already done so, connect with the meeting organizer, panel moderator, and fellow panelists on social media, along with a specific compliment about what they did during the panel discussion. This allows you to build and grow these new relationships.

SHOULD I WRITE A THANK YOU NOTE?

Why not write and send a thank you letter, email, or hand-written note to the meeting organizer, panel moderator, and fellow panelists after participating in a panel discussion? It is a fabulous way to acknowledge all the efforts in an amazing experience on behalf of the audience.

To make your thank you note meaningful, consider these tips:

- **DESCRIPTION.** Believe it or not, some will use these letters as testimonials or references for additional speaking/panel opportunities. Start with a brief description of the panel title, conference name (if appropriate), date, location, and size of the audience.
- **IMPACT.** Describe the overall impact of the panel discussion and the value the overall panel discussion brought to the audience.
- **PERSONAL TOUCH.** Use their name in the salutation. Remember the importance of using a person's name? Add a personal, specific comment about how you felt about the panel, what you learned from the event, and/or your experience working with them.
- **DIFFERENTIATE.** Do not send the same letter to each of them. Take the time to add a noteworthy detail, quote, or insight (or two!) about the contribution they made to the panel discussion.
- **TONE.** Use a warm and sincere tone, considering your relationship with that person. If you know them well, you will be more informal and colloquial. If this is the first time you have worked with them, you might want to be more formal. Keep your writing style natural for you.
- **END ON A POSITIVE NOTE.** Again, thank them for their valuable presence and contribution—and do not forget to actually use those words, "Thank you!" (or some variation).
- **PROMPT.** Send your letter, email, or note as soon after the event as you can. Many prefer to write a draft and then fill in the specifics immediately after the event, so it is fresh in their minds.

By writing a thank you note after the panel discussion, you will create goodwill with the meeting organizer, panel moderator, and fellow panelists. They will probably accept your invitation to LinkedIn, maintain contact, and may even lead to more opportunities in the future. You just never know.

HOW DO I GET ON MORE PANELS?

Congratulations! You had a good experience being a powerful panelist and want to be invited to participate on more panels. Your hard work has paid off in this one panel and you want to do more. That is so exciting!

Here are some ways to parlay your hard work on one panel into invitations to be on more panels:

- **BE A GREAT PANELIST.** Word travels quickly in the meetings industry. It is pretty simple: When you do a great job as a panelist and that panel gets rave reviews from the participants, you will be asked to do more panels.

- **BE EASY.** Not only does the work you do on stage matter, but being easy to work with is just as important. You respond to emails, send in the requested information on time, get to the venue early, and check in with the meeting organizer and panel moderator. No one wants to work with a prima donna.

- **PUBLISH YOUR PERSPECTIVE.** Whether it is in a blog, vlog, LinkedIn article, or YouTube Short, share some learnings that provide insights and value to the prospective audiences.

- **LOOK FOR EVENTS.** Look for other events in your topical space. Look for those events and connect with the event organizers. Let them know that you are interested in being a panelist. They may even publish a "Call for speakers" where you can apply to moderate a panel.

- **LET IT BE KNOWN.** If you do not let others know that you want to do more panels, then only a few people will know you as "the best-kept secret." Let others know, especially those who "hired" you in the past.

- **CREATE PROMOTIONAL MATERIALS.** Clearly state your interest and availability on your social profiles and your website. If you have photos and/or video footage, create a video montage showing your abilities.

- **NURTURE CENTERS OF INFLUENCE.** Consider your colleagues, mentors, and influencers who operate in the space. They do not directly hire panelists, but they know people who do.

- **ASK FOR REFERRALS.** Referral Coach Bill Cates recommends "The bull's eye of referrals is to ask for introductions to specific people. People you know that they know. People in other divisions of the company, sister associations, and you ask, 'How do you feel about introducing me to Laura Jones over at xyz? I would love to meet Laura. From what I can tell, you do similar things. Is that true? If so, could we talk about what that would look like? If you wouldn't mind doing a little email introduction connection, then I can reach out to them. What doesn't usually work is throwing open the whole universe and saying, 'Hey, can you think of anyone else who should know about what I do?'"

- **BE A SPONSOR.** Sometimes, you have to pay to play. Sponsor the panel to get access to the other panelists and/or the audience. Just ask your meeting organizer if they have a sponsorship program. I bet they do!

HOW DO I GET BETTER?

The main way to learn how to be a better panelist is to be a panelist more frequently.

You do know that you will have to do more than that, right? After the panel, note what worked well and what didn't work so great. Then, at the next panel, keep doing what works well and change the things that do not work as well. I realize how basic this sounds, but I am continually surprised at how seldom this happens.

You sit on the panel and then dash off to the next session, meeting, or assignment. Perhaps a bit later, while you are driving home, you think about what worked well and what you would do next time. You *think* you will remember your observations, but you are not on another panel for another few weeks or months, and when it rolls around, you forgot all the things you wanted to do differently!

Here is how I critique myself after a panel or any kind of presentation for that matter:

- **REFLECT.** As soon as possible after the panel, take a moment to reflect on what went well and what did not go so well. Do not forget to consider the feedback received from the panel moderator or meeting organizer as well.
- **ANALYSIS.** Ask yourself these three "W" questions: "What happened?" "Why did that work well?" "Why didn't that work as well as I thought it would?" Your answers could be a host of causes ranging from the format and flow, your approach, and comfort level to the topic and the audience's personality.
- **UPGRADES.** How would you improve your contributions to the panel next time? Write down specifics about how you would change it. Even if you *never* speak on a panel about this topic, still go through this process, as you may give a variation sometime later.
- **ONE THING.** Close to the bottom, draw a red line across the page. Write down the one thing you learned through this critique process. It could be something you want to reinforce or change for the next time.
- **BINDER.** Keep your self-evaluations in a binder or digital folder. As you prepare for your next panel, flip through your binder and notice the trends in your comments, the one thing you learned through the self-evaluation process, and your assessment results. You will notice emerging themes and trends.

For the overachievers reading this book, would you like to get better even faster? You can accelerate your learning curve by watching yourself in action. Record the panel discussion using your smartphone, digital recorder, or ask the A/V tech to record it for you. Do not worry about the digital quality since you are just making this for your own educational benefit and not your YouTube channel.

When watching the recording:

- **MAKE A TRANSCRIPT.** Using speech recognition software, make a transcript of the panel discussion.
- **LISTEN TO YOURSELF.** Notice the language you use. Is it inclusive? Is it descriptive?
    - Could you tell your stories a bit better? Make notations on your transcript as you listen to the panel.
    - Look at your gestures to see if you scrunch or wiggle your eyebrows, wring your hands, crack your knuckles, tap your foot, shift back and forth, sway side to side, blink excessively, or swallow hard or clear your throat
    - Listen for any annoying clicks or vocalized pauses such as "um," "uh," or "like."
- **WATCH YOURSELF.** If you have never watched a video of yourself, this may be a little unsettling, but you will get used to it after you have watched yourself a few times.
    - The first time you watch the video, watch it by yourself with no other objective than to watch yourself. Get the curiosity out of the way.
    - The second viewing should be a thorough critique. Note what worked well and what did not. Try not to get caught up in all the "bad things" you did. Rather, give equal weight to what went well and what you would do differently. Note the significant bits that can be improved on the transcript. Make comments on the side.
    - The third viewing should be with the volume muted. Pay attention to how you are nonverbally connecting with the other panelists and the audience.
    - Finally, watch the video through the audience's eyes. In this case, invite a few friends to watch the video with you (but sit behind them so you do not influence their responses). Note when they become engaged and when they do not. Better yet, videotape the audience rather than (or in addition to) yourself. This way, you will be able to gauge the audience's level of interest.

- **GET ANOTHER PERSPECTIVE.** Though it is helpful to do a self-critique, it is extremely valuable to ask a knowledgeable source to give you objective feedback. The person who is helping you should be a good speaker and someone whose opinion you value. If you can afford it, hire a reputable speech coach who will give you suggestions on how to improve your speaking skills.

CHAPTER SEVEN
VIRTUAL/REMOTE PANELIST TIPS

Virtual panel discussions have revolutionized the way we connect and share ideas, allowing us to engage with people from all over the world in real time. They have opened up new avenues for learning and collaboration that were once impossible, and I believe they will continue to play a critical role in shaping the future of work and education.

Satya Nadella
CEO, Microsoft

Ever since COVID-19 hit the world in 2020, "virtual" panels increased and will continue to grow as we can bring in panelists remotely for in-person, virtual, and hybrid events.

I know. These terms get confusing, so let's start with some definitions:

- A **face-to-face (F2F)** or **in-person** panel discussion is an event where everyone is co-located in the same physical space.
- A **virtual** panel discussion is where everybody is geographically dispersed, connected through a digital platform
- A **hybrid** or **omnichannel** panel discussion is where there is at least one group of people (moderator, panelists, and/or audience) meeting face-to-face while that in-person discussion is streamed or replayed out to geographically dispersed locations.
- A **remote panelist** is a person who is live-streamed to the "main meeting room" in a physical venue or a digital platform

As a remote panelist, consider the possibility that you will have to serve *two* audiences: the in-person and virtual audience(s). You may or may not have to serve both of them at the same time; however, the resulting conversation will decide if, when, and how you will serve them. The meeting organizer may even take recordings (live and replayed) and use them beyond the actual event.

HOW TO BE A BRILLIANT REMOTE PANELIST

Everything written in this book applies to virtual, hybrid, and remote panel experiences. However, you need to recognize some subtle nuances when moving from a F2F environment to a digital environment:

- **PREPARE.** The audience knows when a panelist has just shown up without any thought or preparation. For a virtual panel, your lack of preparation becomes even more obvious. The panelists need to know the overall flow of the conversation and have several key points and takeaways for the audience. Otherwise, the conversation may degrade quickly.
- **BE MORE CONCISE.** Stories and examples need to be tighter and more concise. Succinct headlines are easy ways for people to remember what is being said and repeat it in the chat box. If participating in a special or unique format, best to let the production team know beforehand.
- **BE EQUIPPED.** While your laptop camera is fine, an HD Webcam with good lighting makes for a better user experience. (I trained some panel moderators for Zoom Video Communications, Inc., and they demanded that I go buy one!) Same thing for your audio. An external microphone is ideal.
- **TALK TO THE CAMERA.** Place the camera at eye level and in the middle of the monitor you are looking at during the panel. Yes, sometimes it does get in the way of your screen, but you are building trust with your audience by looking at the camera when you speak. When the camera is off to the side, up or down, it looks like you are distracted.
- **BE ADDITIVE.** Especially in the easily distracted virtual world, the audience does not have the patience for panelists to repeat what other panelists have said. Rather than saying "Yes, I agree with my esteemed colleague," say, "Yes, that is a good point AND [state your new idea]."
- **CONTRIBUTE.** In the F2F world, you can easily signal when you want to speak. In the virtual world, not so much. Even with high-profile executives, our school conditioning kicks in and we awkwardly raise our hands to speak, expecting the panel moderator to call on us! So weird.
- **LEAN IN.** Lean in toward the camera to indicate an interest to speak or consider agreeing ahead of time upon a sign or "tell" when you want to speak. It can even be something as obvious as using the "raised hand"

feature. Then the moderator can easily move the conversation by saying, "[Panelist], looks like you have something you'd like to add!"

- **WHAT TO WEAR.** Recommendations and guidance on what to wear in front of a camera vary. Here are a few simple guidelines:
  - Wear a color contrasting with your background.
  - Jewel tones near your face look best.
  - Beware of wearing black, pastels, and pixilated prints.
  - Wear patterns sparingly.
- **DE-CLUTTER.** Take a preview look at what your audience will see and remove all the detritus behind you including the empty glasses, coffee cups, dead plants, piles of books, folders, and other extraneous stuff that you are not even aware of.
- **TEST THE VIRTUAL BACKGROUND.** Even though virtual backgrounds cover the clutter, test out the background as it may look unprofessional as you move and explosions of color erupt from behind.
- **SILENCE THE AMBIENT NOISE.** Stop the ceiling fan, silence your phone, and turn off your computer notifications. What about the dishwasher, the washing machine, and the dryer? Pets? Kids? They all contribute to the ambient noise distracting the panel.

Like all things moving from F2F into the digital world, it takes a bit more thought and intention. Keep these tips in mind to be a brilliant remote panelist during a virtual or hybrid panel discussion.

HOW TO FOSTER A SENSE OF INTIMACY AS A REMOTE PANELIST

Dr. Ketra Armstrong one of the panelists at TEDxUofM said, "I liked (the Zoom format)...particularly when the cameras are on it feels like there is a level of engagement. If you're in (an actual) panel there's a level of distance, so Zoom brings us close, literally and figuratively."

I agree. The virtual world provides a certain level of intimacy I have not experienced in the in-person world. I think of best-selling author Patrick Lencioni who gave a speech about leadership at the beginning of COVID. As he leaned into the camera, I felt like he was talking just to me.

How do we foster a sense of intimacy over a camera?

- **MINDSET.** First and foremost, get over the idea that virtual is a secondary platform and "not as good" as face-to-face. During the pandemic, virtual was seen more as a substitute and not as good as in-person. Au contraire! It is just different. Our world now consists of *both* modalities. Each has benefits as well as weaknesses. Why not celebrate and leverage the strengths of the virtual platform?

- **BE COMFORTABLE.** You cannot openly share if you are not comfortable - with the platform, the format, the moderator, or your fellow panelists. Take some extra time to go through a tech check, making sure that you are comfortable with the technology. Be proactive and reach out to the panelists and/or moderator. Invest a bit of time to get to know them.

- **TALK TO THE CAMERA.** In the Zoom world, you can look at the gallery view *and* watch yourself. That is so weird when you are trying to have an intimate conversation, especially when your camera is not located in the middle of your computer screen. Please, please, please talk to the camera! To make things easier on yourself, put your camera close to your computer screen or buy a PlexiCam® acrylic webcam holder made specifically to hold your camera in the middle of your computer screen.

- **TALK TO A PERSON.** Intimacy comes from a genuine sense of caring about another human being. As you are talking to the camera, think about one person in that gallery view with whom you want to create that human connection. Simply talk to that person.

- **LEAN IN.** When you are sharing a particularly pertinent point, or sharing something important, lean in like you are telling us a secret. Ahhh...so powerful!

- **TELL PERSONAL AND MEANINGFUL STORIES.** Sharing your story of a struggle that will resonate with the audience, including a few of the tough, real, human emotions that occurred. We can all relate to the struggle and are willing to go on the story-journey with you.

- **MAKE IT ABOUT THEM.** Although you are sharing your story, make it relevant to the audience. When you care about the audience, they will care about what you say.

- **BE GENUINE.** Throughout this "list" to create intimacy, the bottom line is being authentic and genuine in your conversation. Forget this list. Just be you. Speak from the head, heart, and hands. Share the information and stories that your audience cares about and will benefit from.

- **HAVE FUN.** Do not forget to enjoy yourself while you are moderating or being on a panel discussion. When you have fun, so will the audience.

HOW TO SPARK INTEREST REMOTELY

Just as actors and speakers use the physical stage, virtual presenters, panel moderators, and panelists should use the "camera stage" to spark interest and variety while on screen.

Unfortunately, many adopt a restrained "newscaster style" approach to the camera: their headshot is front and center, looking directly at the camera and never moving. While this is not "bad," it can be rather tiresome.

Why not spice up your camera stage with a little variety?

- **CAMERA FRAME.** The traditional "frame" is sitting down with your face in the center of the screen, the camera at eye level, and "one hand" distance between the top of your head and the frame. You do not have to be so stoic:
    - Try standing up, showing more than just your face.
    - Encourage the moderator and panelists to have a "two camera" set up so the person can toggle between different camera views.
- **BACKGROUNDS:**
    - "Stage" your background to look interesting. Room Rater is a clever way to see what works - and what does not.
    - Create a virtual background for each panelist matching their area of expertise.
    - Orchestrate different virtual backgrounds for each panelist matching the segment of the panel. For example, when the panel moves to Q&A, the moderator and panelists all switch their virtual backgrounds.
    - Have a panelist take us on a "tour" of their room, office, or house.
- **POSITION.** In addition to centering yourself on the screen, stand or sit to the right or left of the screen. When performed live, you can put a monitor beside you and show slides, pop up a virtual background that accommodates where your head will be, or when recorded, insert a graphic beside you.
- **MOVEMENT.** As a remote panelist, your movements are limited to within the camera view. You can move closer to the camera when making an important point or sharing a secret with the audience. If you want to move around, place markers (e.g. tape on the floor) in front of the camera so that you know exactly where to stop before you go out of frame.

- **GESTURES.** On stage, gestures are much bigger and broader. After all, you have a whole stage to work with! On camera, your gestures are confined to the camera view, so they are smaller and more nuanced. You want to be a tad bit more animated than normal while still being genuine, enthusiastic, and passionate as the topic matter permits. Smile, nod, or use your hands to create interest. Something as simple as holding up your fingers to note which point you are making goes a long way.
- **NERVOUS TICS.** The camera will pick up facial gestures that you would not normally notice in a F2F performance. Watch a few of your practice recordings to see if you scrunch or wiggle your eyebrows, wring your hands, crack your knuckles, tap your foot, shift back and forth, sway side to side, blink excessively, swallow hard, clear your throat, or utter the proverbial vocalized pauses such as "um," "uh," or "like" too often. Blogger Laci Texter suggests that you "Periodically check in with your body language to see if you are tensing up. Some subconscious signs include crossing your arms, bouncing your leg, gritting your teeth, or forcing a smile."
- **VISUALS.** I am a big fan of using props on stage *and* on camera. Rather than simply talking about it, why not show it? Just make sure you practice how to hold it up to the camera or share your screen.
- **DRESS THE PART.** Alter your appearance so that your audience becomes excited and intrigued with your panel discussion. Just keep in mind that in the virtual world, you will only be visible from the waist up, unless you position your camera otherwise.

Please, do not do ALL of these in the same panel, but one or two techniques will certainly add more pizazz to your panel discussion.

WHAT TO WEAR AS A REMOTE PANELIST

Since we have already covered what to wear on a panel discussion in Chapter Two, let's chat about what to wear as a remote panelist. While the factors to consider when selecting the perfect outfit are the same for in-person as well as for participating remotely, a few distinct differences exist. After all, your profile is projected as a "Hollywood Square" vs. a full view of the entire stage.

- **CONTRAST COLORS.** Wear a color contrasting with the background, especially when using a green screen. If you use a virtual background, do a trial run to make sure your silhouette does not flicker when you move. Smooth away those flyaway hairs with a bit of hair cream or spray.

- **POP OF INTEREST.** Add a bit of interest or intrigue with your shirt, tie, scarf, pocket scarf, necklace, or brooch.
- **FIT RIGHT.** Make sure your clothes fit properly. For the most attractive clothing shape for video, choose tailored, form-fitting "toppers." Fashion show producer, Amy Olsen says, "If your tops still appear loose on camera, you can pull a fashion-show production trick and tuck excess fabric behind your back and into your waistband." In the Zoom world, you would be amazed at what a bobby pin or clothespin can do to bring in extra fabric.
- **DO A QUICK CHECK.** Look for visual distractions including loose buttons and threads, visible undergarments, sweat stains, and distracting/noisy jewelry. Do not forget to remove the clutter/distractions in your background, and keep children and pets quiet.
- **GET INSPIRED.** Watch a few news shows and see what the hosts and guests wear. You are bound to pick up some ideas and inspiration.
- **MAKEUP.** Yes, men and women need to pay attention to the savageries of high-definition cameras. Zoom has a function called "Touch up my appearance," which you should definitely turn "on."

TIPS FOR WOMEN

I honestly believe that men have less to worry about on a Zoom panel discussion, whereas women have many more options. Here are a few tips for women as well:

- **COLOR.** Jewel tones near your face look best. Sapphire blue, emerald green, amethyst purple—the more vibrant, the better.
- **FRAME YOUR FACE.** Retailer M.M. LaFleur encourages you to "Frame your face. Details like pretty collars and notched necklines put the emphasis where it should be—on your mouth and the words emanating from it). While a super-low plunge is a no-no, a deep V-neck can draw eyeballs upward to your face."
- **ACCESSORIES.** Wear one eye-catching detail to your blouse or accessory, such as a necklace, earrings, or pin.
- **MAKEUP.** Use foundation and concealer along with a dark lipstick that makes you feel confident. Do not use pink or mauve as they provide low contrast.

Remember, you want people to pay attention to what you are saying rather than be distracted by what you are wearing. Follow these tips on what to wear as a remote panelist and you will definitely impress the audience.

CHAPTER EIGHT
BIGGEST MISTAKES & BEST PRACTICES

The best practices are those that have been tried and tested, refined, and improved over time. They represent the accumulated wisdom of those who have tackled similar challenges before us. By following these practices, we can save ourselves from the pain of reinventing the wheel and avoid common pitfalls.

Indra Nooyi, Former CEO of PepsiCo
Milken Institute Global Conference Panel

In summary, to be a successful panelist requires you to do some things and avoid doing other things. Here is my list of the top ten mistakes panelists make, as well as panelist "do's & don'ts" collected over three decades of moderating panel discussions.

TOP TEN COMMON PANELIST MISTAKES

In a 2014 survey of 539 executives, thought leaders, and meeting planners, 66 percent of the respondents had issues with the panelists being out of control. That is 2/3 of the people think the panelists can do a better job sharing their wisdom with the crowd. After all, how hard can it be for a panelist to show up, share a few pearls of wisdom, and answer a few questions?

Being a powerful panelist takes more than just showing up. Here are the top ten most common mistakes panelists make during a panel discussion, and what you can do about them:

1. **DOMINATED THE DISCUSSION/ANSWERED EVERY QUESTION.** This requires the panelist to be self-aware of how much airtime they are using. Be considerate of your fellow panelists and do not hog the airtime. Even if you have something worthwhile to add to the conversation, if you have been dominating, try

deflecting an answer to another suitable panelist - or even out to the audience.

2. **PROMOTED THEMSELVES/THEIR COMPANY.** Crossing the fine line between mentioning that your book was just released and hawking the darn thing by picking it up and lovingly petting it like your long-lost puppy. Avoid mentioning that people can buy it at any online or local bookseller and telling them they would be idiots if they did not come up to talk to you about the book etc. Here is the hard truth: the audience is not stupid. They know who you are and what company you work for. Provide great value and takeaways for the audience and then you and your company may bask in the afterglow. If you rocked the house, people will come up to talk to you about the book you casually mentioned once.

3. **GOT OFF TOPIC/DID NOT MAKE THE POINT.** Nobody likes a rambler. Stick to the topic and the question being discussed. Make your answers pithy and to the point. Everyone likes a good story, just make sure it is tightly told *and* relevant to the point.

4. **WAS NOT CONVERSATIONAL.** Perhaps the "panel discussion" was a series of presentations, or the panelists did not listen to the question or each other, or perhaps they did not build on what each person was saying to create a conversation. Part of this is the responsibility of the moderator, but every panelist is allowed to make it more conversational by really being present and listening to their fellow panelists. Contribute to the conversation by bridging key points and making a new statement. Ask another panelist for his or her opinion. Think of the session as a lively dinner table conversation!

5. **DISAGREEABLE.** Some panelists are just going to argue about everything…and do not argue with me about that! LOL! Seriously, just do not be *that* person.

6. **REPETITIVE.** Panelists who repeat what has already been said are annoying. "Yes, I agree with Sally" and then spend two minutes paraphrasing what Sally just said. What a waste of time! Try saying, "I agree with Sally AND…" then add something *new* to the conversation. Or try saying, "I agree with Sally BUT…." and then mention a specific upgrade you have to her thinking. Be *additive* to the conversation and not *repetitive*.

7. **POOR SPEAKING/PRESENTATION SKILLS.** You would never just show up to give an important speech, so why would you just show up to serve on a panel? Do some prep work thinking through your key messages and prepare a handful of talking points with a short story illustrating each point. Think of it as a media interview where your words need to be more of a soundbite than a long-drawn-out lecture. If you fear public speaking, consider getting a coach to help you be a better panelist.

8. **SUPERFICIAL COMMENTS.** The audience wants the inside scoop, real takeaways, and powerful insights, not some fluffy comments of no value. Make sure your talking points are meaningful and relevant to that specific audience.

9. **APPEAR DISTRACTED.** Going somewhere? Stop looking at your watch, picking at your shoes, or glancing away from the action. You look (and probably are) distracted. Stay present in the moment and be self-aware of your situation. The moderator is keeping track of time and you have every expectation that the session will end on time.

10. **ARRIVED LATE.** Take into account the traffic and other maladies that can torpedo your day and arrive at least a few minutes early to touch base with the moderator and fellow panelists. Warm yourself up by mingling with the crowd. Get a sense of what is on their minds so you can address their concerns appropriately.

You can view the entire report at this QR code.

11 THINGS A PANELIST SHOULD DO

1. **SERVE THE AUDIENCE.** The audience paid good money (at the very least invested their time) to be there, so speak to them and not just each other. Figure out what they want to know from you and then serve it up. Help them solve problems and find solutions. Anticipate their questions, and have answers and resources ready.

2. **CHECK-IN WITH THE MODERATOR.** Speak to the moderator well beforehand to align your expectations. Find out who the other panelists are, why you were chosen, and what role you play. Ask for the format of the program along with a working agenda, speaking order, and ground rules. Finally, ask how best to support each other. At the very least, the moderator will ask for a short bio that is interesting and relevant as well as some pithy, provocative questions about the topic.

3. **BE PREPARED.** Always keep the audience in mind as you research the other panelist's positions and determine what makes you/your position unique from the others. Be ready to introduce yourself succinctly (2-3 sentences are

great) and share 3-5 key messages that matter. Be ready to support your points with concrete examples and crisp, concise stories to humanize your message and drive it home. Think of a quick sound bite that everyone will write down because it is so cool—and so right!

4. **BE TIMELY.** Show up on time, even a little bit early. Then, stick to your time limits. For example, if you are given five minutes to present, take four minutes to share with a sentence to recap. It is all about respecting the audience and following the prescribed process.

5. **FOLLOW THE MODERATOR'S LEAD.** Hopefully, you will have a good moderator who provides clear instructions. Speak when invited and give signals to the moderator when you would like to contribute to the discussion.

6. **BE HONEST.** Your audience wants insider information. They may be struggling with topical issues that you successfully conquered. As you share your ideas, be honest about your struggles, what worked as well as what did not. Be open, honest, and a little humble too.

7. **USE THE MICROPHONE.** When working with only one microphone for all the panelists, make sure you have ready access to it. Lift it close to your mouth and speak confidently into it while looking at the audience.

8. **TAG ON.** Have a conversation rather than a ping-pong match between the moderator and individual panelists by making explicit links or references to what other panelists have said. Add to or disagree with their contributions by saying "Let me add something to that idea…" or "We take a different approach at our company…" Be additive and not repetitive to the discussion, and do not feel compelled to answer every question, especially when another panelist gave a perfectly fine answer.

9. **DISAGREE DIPLOMATICALLY.** At some point, you *will* disagree with the other panelists, otherwise, why have a panel discussion? One of the panelists will say something that is not consistent with your own view or perspective. You have got to weigh in! Respectfully disagree without being disagreeable. Rather than saying "Jacob, that's stupid," respond by saying something like "Jacob, I understand how your research could lead you to infer this; however, my fieldwork indicates otherwise."

10. **ENJOY YOURSELF.** If you are having fun, the audience will too. Smile. Laugh. Tease each other in a kindhearted way. Your audience wants you to succeed, so show your passion and enthusiasm for the topic. Just relax; it will all be over in an hour or so!

11. **MAKE FRIENDS.** You have the opportunity to create great relationships with your fellow panelists, moderator, and audience members, particularly if you were articulate and made relevant points. Being a panelist is a great way to connect with other high-profile experts so do not hesitate to follow up with an email and continue the conversation.

11 THINGS A PANELIST SHOULD *NOT* DO

1. **DON'T WING IT.** You have to do more than just show up. Audiences are expecting a scintillating conversation similar to their experiences on CNN or Fox News. Great panelists take the time to think through the key messages, headlines, and inspiring (and concise) stories—otherwise, you may end up looking like a fool from the Jerry Springer Show.

2. **DON'T BE BORING.** Yes, your job is to educate, but you must also be entertaining. Show your energy and enthusiasm for the subject. Have a few interesting facts, real stories, and illustrative examples and keep it short. No more than 90 seconds is a good goal. People prefer snappy, well-thought-out answers to interesting questions. If you are able, try to make things a bit humorous—but leave out the joke about how many panelists it takes to screw in a lightbulb!

3. **DON'T GET HUFFY.** In a good panel, you will be interrupted, challenged, and contradicted. The moderator will cut you off if you go over time. You do not have to answer every question. You will not always get in the last word. Let it go. Be gracious to others and they will be gracious to you.

4. **DON'T BE A JERK.** Do not cut off other panelists or the moderator. Do not interrupt in the middle of another panelist's remarks. Do not hog the spotlight. Balance your airtime with others on the panel and give everyone a chance to weigh in and answer questions.

5. **DON'T USE SLIDES.** Can you show a prop or a physical model? Put the information in a handout? Give the audience a link to further information? If you must, use one or two slides requiring a visual representation of a key idea—a graph, chart, or image—and the audience should not have to squint to read it.

6. **DON'T SHAMELESSLY SELF-PROMOTE.** Some panelists just cannot help themselves pitching their product, service, or company. Do not be that person. NO ONE wants to hear your sales pitch. Instead, make your comments in service to the audience, and at the end, let them know you are available afterward to discuss the panel topic further.

7. **DON'T BE A CONTRARIAN.** Yes, disagreements are to be expected but do not disagree simply because you can. Disagree because the discussion will benefit the audience *and* your reputation.

8. **DON'T THINK NO ONE IS LOOKING.** Even though you are not speaking, the audience will be watching you. Stay poised and professional. Look at the other panelists when they are talking. Do not sigh, eye-roll, zone out, scratch, cross and uncross your legs, or fiddle with your smartphone or laptop.

9. **DON'T FAKE IT.** If you do not know the answer to the question, simply say so. Do not ramble or make something up. Somebody is recording your response to post on YouTube immediately after the panel is over. If someone else on the panel might be able to answer the question, punt it over by saying, "I have never experienced this myself, but perhaps Jacob has some ideas on this?"

10. **DON'T PONTIFICATE.** Do not talk down to or lecture the audience. This is a discussion, not a dissertation. You are having a conversation with the other panelists and the audience as colleagues, not to serve your ego.

11. **DON'T DISTRACT.** Be aware of your physical presence, especially if you are on a raised platform, sitting on comfortable chairs without a table in front of you. Short skirts, plunging necklines, dangly jewelry, shoes with worn soles, and shoes worn with no socks distract the audience from the message. It does not add to your credibility, either.

You can download a these panelist do's and don'ts at this QR code.

CONCLUSION

I hope you are now fortified with information and inspired to be the absolute best, most awesome panelist at your upcoming panel discussion. Perhaps you have another question to ask or an idea to share that will help your fellow panelists. Please share it with me at www.PowerfulPanels.com. You can also:

- Check out our resources and checklists to help you prepare for your next panel discussion at www.PowerfulPanels.com.

- Continue the conversation at our LinkedIn Powerful Panels group.

- Access our FREE (and who doesn't like free?) 7-part video e-course at www.PowerfulPanels.com. It is full of tips and techniques that professional moderators rely on. These short training videos will take you through, step by step, to moderating a lively and engaging panel discussion at any meeting, conference, or convention. With your course registration, you will receive several bonus templates and checklists.

- Listen to our podcast: *Powerful Panels*—available on Apple, Stitcher, and Spotify—where we opine about all things regarding panel discussions.

- Subscribe to my YouTube channel to receive a weekly *Powerful Panel Discussion Tip*.

- Read my two other books on panels: Powerful Panels: A Step-by-Step Guide to Moderating Lively and Informative Panel Discussions at Meetings, Conferences and Conventions and 123 Ways to Add Pizazz to a Panel Discussion. You can order yours online at Amazon or www.PowerfulPanels.com.

- Unlock the Powerful Panels Knowledge Vault—a compilation of best practices of some of the most successful professional panel moderators. It is chock-full of customizable checklists, worksheets, templates, scripts, specialty format agendas, sample emails, PowerPoint templates, video examples of the good, the bad, and the ugly, video interviews with industry icons and professional moderators, recorded webinars and slideshows, industry reports on the effectiveness of panels and more.

- Hire me to coach you to moderate a lively and informative panel discussion or be a powerful panelist

- Bring me in to train your team of moderators or panelists.

- Or, just have me moderate your next panel discussion.

Please join me in my crusade to make all panel discussions powerful and extraordinary. If you want to share a tip, technique, or reaction to something you learned while reading this book, I would be honored to hear from you at kristin@PowerfulPanels.com.

ACKNOWLEDGEMENTS

None of these techniques were created in a vacuum. I either observed them over the years or was inspired by others. Specifically, I would like to thank these folks who have graciously allowed me to ask questions, probe into the process, and capture various techniques for this book: Patrick Allen, Tom Antion, Ketra Armstrong, Katie Azevedo, Barry Banther, Bill Cates, Trevor Currie, Jan Fox, Pam Fox Rollin, Cathy Fyock, Sylvie di Giusto, David Greenberg, Adam Guild, Chip Heath, Sasscer Hill, Timothy Hyde, Jennifer B. Kahnweiller, Frank Kelly, Shola Kaye, Pam Leinmiller, Lisa Marshall, Lea McLeod, Jo Miller, John Molidor, Kristina Moore, David Morin, Amy Olson, Mike Peiru, Rosemary Ravinal, Alan Stevens, Mark Suster, Laci Texter, Kay Thrace (not her real name), and Brian Walter.

A shout oout to my editor, Lorraine Bossé-Smith who strived to make the book grammatically correct. I take complete responsibility for the final product. Not her fault if you see something wonky!

Another thank you to my retired friend and neighbor, Susan Stark, who inspired this book when reading this book's predecessor, *123 Ways to Add Pizazz to a Panel Discussion*. My heart sang when she said, "If I had only read this book when I was a working professional. I had no idea you could do all that with a panel!"

Finally, my biggest inspiration comes from you: the current and future panelists of the world. We desperately need to upgrade the panel experience. You now have a guidebook to help you be even more comfortable and confident than ever!

ABOUT THE AUTHOR

KRISTIN ARNOLD, MBA, CSP, CPF|MASTER is a high-stakes meeting facilitator and professional panel moderator. She has been facilitating teams of executives and managers in making better decisions and achieving greater results for over 30 years. She is known for her concrete approach to teamwork and a treasure trove of practical concepts, tools, and techniques her clients can apply immediately to see positive, substantive results.

One of her favorite formats for helping executives, experts, and practitioners share their ideas with others is the panel discussion at meetings, conferences, and conventions.

She is a leading authority on moderating panel discussions, has been heralded by MeetingsNet as the *Panel Improvement Evangelist,* and recognized as a meetings innovator by *Smart Meetings Magazine.* Her article in *Toastmasters Magazine* continues to be their top-rated article and a lead article in organic Google searches. She is the author of the definitive book on how to moderate a panel: *Powerful Panels: A Step-by-Step Guide to Moderating a Lively and Informative Panel Discussion at Meetings, Conferences, and Conventions.*

Kristin is one of the first female graduates of the US Coast Guard Academy and the first woman stationed onboard the USCGC Buttonwood, a seagoing buoy tender. She parlayed her understanding of teams and teamwork with an MBA in marketing strategy into a specialized management consulting firm focused on building extraordinary teams in the workplace.

OTHER BOOKS BY KRISTIN ARNOLD

Powerful Panels
A Step-by-Step Guide to Moderating a Lively and Informative Panel Discussion at Meetings, Conferences and Conventions

123 Ways to Add Pizazz to a Panel Discussion

Boring to Bravo
Proven Presentation Techniques to Engage, Involve and Inspire Your Audiences to Action

Team Basics: Practical Strategies for Team Success

Team Energizers: Practical Team Activities

Email Basics: Practical Tips to Improve Team Communication

Kristin's books are available with special discounts for bulk purchases. Customized editions with personalized covers and forewords, printed excerpts of existing books, and white-labeled products can be created for specific events or organizations.

Please contact Kristin for complete information
800.589.4733 • 480.399.8489
kristin@PowerfulPanels.com • www.PowerfulPanels.com

Please visit our site for additional content and frequent updates.